A Long Shot Literary Lions Publication

About Long Shot Literary Lions

Renowned poet Maya Angelou taught us that the caged bird sings because it has something to say. In that same spirit, Long Shot Literary Lions is a publishing entity that firmly believes that there are many incarcerated individuals who are gifted, talented and have something to say. We are committed to helping to tell the profound truths and captivating stories of those who are incarcerated physically; yet with a message that penetrates beyond physical bars.

Many incarcerated individuals are uncertain of how to get their works published; or unclear as to whom they can entrust their stories to in order to complete the process. Oftentimes believing that it is merely a "long shot" which won't succeed; most of them often give up on the process.

On the other hand, you have those who are *literary lions*. These individuals are fierce in spirit and believe in the positive messages they possess so much that they are willing to persevere until that message is told. Consequently, when you are reading the poems, prose and narratives that are crafted on these pages, you are beholding the message of *literary lions* who "took a shot" and made it!

The Prisoners' Pen: Poems of Pain, Passion & Purpose

The Prisoners' Pen is a collection of poems from current and formerly incarcerated individuals. It possesses various forms of poetic expression that give voice to the many facets of mass incarceration. The levels range from personal expressions of regret and pain to pointed messages of redemption. Told by the pen of more than 20 different poets, this work of art is sure to either pierce your soul or provoke your consciousness.

It is important to note that all ***of the contributing poets have agreed that they will not personally profit from the proceeds of this book.*** Instead, the proceeds will be used to benefit children of incarcerated parents and ministries/organizations that support families of incarcerated individuals.

The Literary Lions

C.W. Fleming

Ata The Lion

Clinton T. Berry

L. Brown

Kevin Burns

Rodney Cash

Melvin Davis

Deshaun

King David Dunn

Damion Ford

Charles Green

Griffen

S. Hall

Reginald Hicks, Sr.

Randall Hutcherson

Hope

Alan Jackson

J. Hood

Elmer J. Lockett, Jr.

Markiet Logging, Sr.

Myron Lovings

Antong Lucky

Jeff McClendon

Willie Joe McAdams

WC McMullin

Torrick McMurray Sr.

Henry Molina

Peek

Kielyn Reed

Rico

Carlton S.

Osborne Scott

Oscar Stephen III

Joseph Torrey

Calvin T. Trahan

Jacob Van De Carr

Lion M. O'Neil

Foreword

Behind this book is a small crowd of people who, over the course of many months and even years, worked together throughout different parts of the prison to break down racial barriers, class distinctions, affiliations and associations along with our editor and publisher on the phone to turn this idea into a vision.

This work of art conceived and created in solitude is carried forth by a team passing through many hands before it reaches the marketplace

So that once in the marketplace it can help the children and the families we left behind.

We thank all who have purchased, laughed, cried contemplated and hold our words dear to their heart.

And we thank the unmentioned hands who helped this book become a reality.

Table of Contents

Poems of Pain

Poems of Passion

Poems of Purpose

Poems for Our Children

A Message from W. Fleming

I take pride in presenting this work to the world. It is a humble collaboration of current and ex-prisoners who love poetry and continue to use it as a vehicle to express frustrations, pain, loss, love, redemption and hope.

Its collaboration took convincing and time. There were many walks in the gym, talks on the rec-yard, hours on the phone, and impromptu poetic discussions in the chow hall and rewrites in the infirmary. However, we came together to share our love and our gift and to commit it to the children we left behind and the ministries that minister to us.

Many of the poems penned under the name C.W. Fleming are in fact true stories of other brothers who wanted to participate but didn't write poetry I am thankful for them allowing me to pen their stories and or feelings.

Special thanks to my "Spoken Word Wizards" Kielyn Reed and Joseph Torrey who shared their skills and work unselfishly. I also want to thank Edmond Davis, who created an artistic expression which truly captured the essence of The Prisoners' Pen: Poems of Pain, Passion and Purpose.

This work is an anthology that represents the many varied subjects of our life in here, the families that support us, and our issues with the system, politics and each other. However, this book is not an anti-anything book; but meant to capture realness and the truth is in every poem.

Inmates influence inmates more than anyone else. We hope that this collaboration will influence other brothers and sisters in the system to write. We hope that the administration will begin to host writing seminars and think tanks for those who are in college as well as those who have no formal education.

We also want to send a forever shout out to Dr. Terri LeClercq for being a tireless advocate of inmate writings and readings without censorship.

Lastly, I want to thank The "C" in C.W. Fleming. My wife, soulmate, best-friend, and co-author. Thanks for all the rewrites, edits, graphic work, reading over the phone, personal financial investments and belief in the *"Long Shot Literary Lions"* that has in the end brought this work to fruition. You are the inspiration behind every unction that ignites my imagination and the hands that delivers it to manifestation.

Why We Write – *Kielyn Reed*

Atonement by articulation

Relentlessly striving for reconciliation

Motivated by love and faith

Inspired while sitting in the midst of hate

Governed with love and founded in truth

Detaching from those who live in abuse

Who are we?

Self-portrayed lions contained to our dens

Casting long literary shots with the thrust of our pens

Once outcast, now outspoken

Once outrageous, now outshining

Some were almost broken

Until one day when God started mining

Who are we?

Present prisoners pursuing a purpose while pushing our pens

Men who have been debased and deprived

Yet found a reason to survive

By injecting words of faith, hope and love into others' lives.

We fight away insanity with our daily pleas to society

We are the 2.3 million

Who have committed some type of crime against society

A paralyzed parent who happens to be a prisoner

That's armed with only a piece of paper and a pen

The ignored intelligent adolescent that evolved after twenty-four years

of incarceration into the informed inmate who everyone considers a

friend.

Condemned to die in prison as a consequence of the crimes he
committed
Yet he now spends his time composing conscientious collaborations
with other convicts.
Why we write...
The one thing we all have in common is our need to reach out beyond
the walls that contain us
They confine our creativity, our compassion and our chance to share
the wisdom that can only be found in the pits of transgression
We fight to write and we write to fight
For the families we lost
For the women we've loved
For the people we've hurt
For the forgiveness we long for.
Writing is our way to escape the madness and the sadness of living in
a cage
Maya once wrote, "Why does the caged bird sing?"
The answer-
It was the only way to express their pain.
We write for the father that never got a chance to raise his son or
daughter
For the mother that was separated from her child at birth
We write because words transcend all walls, transform all
understanding and transport minds to different places.
We write for the lost love of poetry that has the power to heal the
world's ills.

If the world was formed with words, then it just might be the lack of kind words that we should share with each other that's causing so much misery.

We write...we write...we write.

For the parents, politicians and leaders who are desperately searching for the answers to the problems that plague our communities.

We know the answers because we were the reasons for the problems in society.

We write to fight social retardation- and social discord that's destroying our nation.

We write because that's the only thing we have to give

To a world we hope that can find the capacity to forgive

We write to offer solutions for the pollutions we helped to create

We write to emancipate the image that all prisoners are consumed by hate

We write because it's important for the words of those who have committed a mistake to be resounded into society; if only to awake the youngsters who acknowledge only those who once live by the code of the streets.

We must correct the fable that there's glamour and honor with incarceration and the game.

So take a trip into the Lion's den where we write for every reason other than fame.

Pain

"There is no birth of consciousness without pain." – Carl Jung

Pain- *Kielyn Reed*

It's like living in vain when you're watching it rain,

yet it's impossible for you to touch.

Seems like your soul is crying when all your family is dying

and your heart is screaming, "Too much."

The other day I saw so much gray in my mother's hair.

What's even more depressing is the fact that I "know I put it there.

Incarcerated at the age of eighteen due to chasing gutter dreams of things

thatbling

Neverknew thepain those things wouldbring

Untiltheconcreteandbarsstarteddrivingmeinsane

I left my lady with a baby that grew up to hate me. While she's struggling to

feed two, she was crying, *"Baby I need you."*

But what can a man do when his hands turn blue from being

handcuffed

away from the life he's trying to pursue?

Now the son I left to fend for his self has somehow succumb to the streets

and drugs.

At any rate its fate that felt the need to imitate his most ‑hated thug.

For months and days I cried and wrote unanswered letters to my young

self

Then one day I was called to the chapel

and told about my eighteen yearold son's death

I know she still loves me

I really want to believe that she still cares.

Yet when I reach out to her loving embrace there's no one

standing there

The letters stopped years ago and all my pictures has started to fade

Yet, it turned your smile into a frown with all the bad decisions that

I've made

So imagine my reaction when your letter came that day

All my anticipation was over and I couldn't wait to read what you had
to say
Eighteen words in one sentence was all you wrote to me saying-
"I know you and I were meant to be;
but that's all in the past because you're not free."
You're the most beautiful part of me
The most persistent and secure base I ever had.
You're the center of my universe being my friend, mother and dad.
Carried me for nine months, protected me for seventeen years, then
supported me through twenty years of incarceration
You're my divine peace of mind that will always be my inspiration
That's why I'll never forget the day that my world came to an end
When I was told by a complete stranger that I had lost my best friend
Pain in which we all express the perpetual grief our souls endure
Pain is the name of the constant silhouette that follows us day to year
Pain is universal, unoccupied, unfriendly and unhealthy
Yet on lock it's all we've got
So bask into the pain of the numerous men who have been cast
into massive caged warehouses to rot and be forgotten.
Warehouses that its dwellers call
The House of Pain!

Fist Full of Tears-

by Incarcerated Veteran Jeff McClendon, US Air Force Firefighter

Why do we all walk around here acting like everything is okay

When deep down inside, our hearts are rotting like tooth decay

As soldiers we've been taught and told not to show our emotions

We just keep to ourselves until a woman can squeeze them out like a
bottle of lotion

What's up with us?

Is it our pride, our shame our egos or our fears

That won't let us relax and release our fist full of tears

We sit here in our cells reminiscing about our past

Wondering where did I go wrong should I have seen this coming?

It seems like everything just happened so fast

I have gone from a productive citizen, a soldier who honorable fought
for his country

To becoming just a number – or worse- an offender- the scumbag of
the earth to say it bluntly

It's a struggle everyday living with this post-traumatic stress

The nightmares, having thoughts of suicide, waking up in cold sweats

I've tried so many ways to cope with this throughout the years

But the best theory I've discovered is releasing my fist full of tears

Sometimes I get upset watching the political propaganda of TV

Honestly, I feel like the military left me hanging- they didn't even try
to help me

How could you send someone in a jungle filled with silverback
gorillas?

And expect him to survive without becoming a stone-cold killer

We just want to adjust back into society, and be proudly looked upon by our peers

But on the inside we know something else is wrong and we can't release our fist full of tears

When you feel like you're all alone and emotionally neglected

Walking around with a fist full of tears make you feel protected

It's hiding your emotions so that no one else will notice

And still trying to remain sane and 100% focused

When you're smiling on the outside, but internally you're in anguish

It's like you're screaming for help, but no one can understand your language

What I can say is only the strongest of soldiers will survive and conquer our biggest fears

So I guess I gotta man up, get on my knees, catch my breath

And open my fist full of tears

This Experience - *Jacob T. Van De Carr*

This experience
Has made me laugh and
made me cry

This experience
Is just an effective dream
that will soon pass by

This experience
Has gotten my attention and
caught my mind's eye

This experience
No longer has me
questioning what, where
when and why

This experience
Has humbled me and
vanquished my pride
This experience
For the truth can no longer
be denied

This experience

Has revealed the Everlasting
One as my guide

This experience
Gives me my appreciation for
life and love to be shared far
and wide
This experience...

My Shame – *Joseph Torrey*

A mother too busy to love
Partying and on drugs
Paved the way for me
Being a thug
So I confused camaraderie
With love
And gravitated toward
Everything else
Opposite of it
And all of the above
That the streets had to offer
Like
High speed chases
Gang ties
And capital cases
Caught by cats telling me
That it was cool to commit
felonies
And lame to win spelling
bees
So I disregarded formal
education
To learn how to rob and start
selling D
Brought up and caught up in
a ball of confusion
until I came to the
conclusion
that what appeared to be real
was all an illusion

The Unforgiven Self –
C.W. Fleming

It dizzied me that you visited
me
You shouldn't have come
I'm an embarrassment
A bum
I'm worse than dumb
I did everything that they say
I did
I even killed a kid
I don't like myself. I despise
and loathe myself. I will
never forgive myself
Life without parole is not a
deep enough hole
I should be where there is no
dirt. Never to live again on
planet Earth
I'm sorry that you gave me
birth
I release you of all your pain
Tell the family that all the
drinking drove me insane
The alcohol had taken
control of my will
Long before I got behind the
wheel

Nothing can justify my kills

Don't think that I don't feel
the lost souls of the family
that I killed
Please erase me from your
mind and know that I'll be
trying to die before the end of
my time.
Man!

Love Always-
C.W.Fleming

I enjoyed our visit
Although you seemed
uncomfortable and
rigid
I will stand beside you
as you do your time
I have already forgiven
you for your crime
I know it's the biggest
mistake you ever made
A life sentence is a hard
debt to be paid
But I'm not undone by
what you've done
I will never forsake or
leave you- because you
are my son
So unless I write and
tell you otherwise
I'll be to visit again this
weekend right after the
sunrise.

My Name is Michelle-
C.W. Fleming

At first I didn't know that I
was being abused
He was my father so at seven
I was confused
At night he would lay on top
of me under the covers
I would feel extreme pain
and smothered
It would always end with his
laugh and liquored kiss
And a promise to get me
anything I wished
My mother wasn't there and
my stepmother didn't care
she was abused by him too
Beating us up seemed to be
the only thing he could do
He became more vicious as
his sexual demands became
more twisted
My inability to perform them
kept my lip blistered
By the time I was eleven I
was his nightly sex toy
He broke my jaw with a
pistol for looking at a boy

When he was finally caught
He said it was my fault
For all of his abominations
He only got ten years of
probation
Thirty years have passed and
I am still suffering from my
past
Because of my childhood
abuse- life has really been
hard
My only refuge has been the
Lord
That's the truth of my life
that I must tell
From age seven to fourteen I
lived through hell. *My name
is Michelle.*

The Least – *C.W. Fleming*
The least of us all don't have
cell phones that you can call
Those left behind can't pay
for the psychotropic meds to
stabilize their minds
So they medicate their self
with wine
Or sometimes
Marijuana, cocaine, heroin,
Xanax or "X"
Their issues are complex
They have already been put
out of their apartment
complex
So they hustle, steal and
prostitute
Their real problem is that
they are unemployable and
destitute
Across the country their
number has risen
The taxpayers' solution has
been prison
But of course
That was a bad decision
For them- prison didn't work
They came out far worse and
hurt

We who believe need to be
alert
Those are our brothers and
sisters sleeping under the
bridge in the dirt
Please hear and heed their
call
They truly are the least of us
all
Some of them are too weak
and small
To be exposed to the extreme
elements of the weather
It doesn't make any sense for
this to be happening in our
Great America

Unnamed- *C.W. Fleming*

I'm the son of man so it took
me a while to understand
That I can only grow holding
on to God's unbreakable
hand
I've made mistakes- fell flat
on my face
Never would have made it
without Grace
Now that I've returned home
I find that I'm not alone
As everyone cries as they sing
new worship songs
Some are speaking in
tongues
Others are teaching The
Word to the young
While others are on their
knees seeking repentance for
all they've done
It keeps me teary-eyed and
humble;
Yet thankful to be in the
number that has began to
ponder
How God's love truly is the
World's greatest wonder.

One of Those- *C.W. Fleming*

If your eyes were closed
Would you think that I am
one of those whose character
is defined by designer clothes
and talking about Van Gohs?
Or would I be one of those
whose face shows his woes
And who seems to care less
about other peoples' lows?
Or would you consider me
one of those who regularly
attends Broadway shows
And opine about the lyrical
rhyme of Edgar Allen Poe
Or would you patiently wait
to hear my prose
To dissect what my mind
knows
To determine if I am one of
those
Who is worthy of your heart's
rose
As it goes, you could suppose
That I am neither of those
and yet still deserving to be
chose
With your eyes closed
Am I one of those?

Needles & Spoons-
Randall Hutcherson

This is a debt of the heart
that need not be seen; lose
the needle and spoon before
you find out exactly what I
mean.
It's a one way trip to a dark
place in hell
The pit is so deep one begins
to think that God can't hear
them yell.
Dying with a needle in your
arm isn't at all the curse
It's living with the needle in
your arm that's a hundred
times worse
You'll be lost and confined in
a dark hidden cellar
That you will wish you had
never known
Once in there you will cry
like a baby from the
humiliation, demonic
cravings and longings to
return home.

You may think that you're all
that and have things under
control
But the needle and spoon
have broken the boldest of
the bold and left them dead
under a bench in the cold.
You start off thinking you
can handle it like you're and
exception to the rule
But you end up a statistic
that's sick and selling their
soul and feeling like a brand
new damned fool.
The needle and spoon started
you off thinking that they
were your friend
All the while they were
escorting you to a bitter and
bedeviled end.
It's not the last shot of dope
that kills a man
It's the first shot usually
injected by a foreign hand.
The needle and spoon is
certain death in slow motion
It's the devil's personally
created poison potion.

The freedom you seek can
only be found with God
After the first three days it
won't be hard.
After 21 days you'll be free
and singing in tune
Mercifully escaping the death
of the needle and spoon.

You're in the Pen- *C.W. Fleming*

You're in the pen and my
whole world feels like it's
coming to an end
I just wake up some
mornings mad
For no good reason
Your son just wakes up
acting bad
The new baby is always
crying
My grandmother was just
told that she is dying
My job is trying to get me to
do stuff that I ain't buying
Everybody but us is having
money in the south
Your mama just got put out
of her house
Trump is in the White House
And you're in the pen
The police done started back
capping
The Movement is finally
happening
Jay-Z done started back
rapping
And you're in the pen

For the first time I am
invited to a family reunion
with your kin
And you're in the pen
Amber has broken her water
She needs to know that her
life matters
Your sister came by the
house looking beaten and
battered
And you're in the pen
I got a ticket the other day
I already got too many bills
to pay
Last week was my birthday
Today is Valentine's Day
Just something I had to say
And you're in the pen
All the red check engine
lights are on in the ride
The pastor is looking at me
funny cause I ain't paid tithes
Your baby mama and me are
about to collide
And you're in the pen
Then only good news came
by way of the phone
I've won a six day all
expenses paid trip to Rome

The sad news is I got to take
my girlfriend
Because you're in the pen
Now don't start acting hood
Cause I'm good
I'll be by your side until this
is over because I'm your wife,
friend and lover
I'm just letting you know
how hard it's been
Since you've been in the pen.

Odyssey- *Rodney Keith*
Cash
Fifteen years old, I
had barely been born
I didn't think that one day I
would have to weather a
storm
In my youth I wouldn't listen
I also had a father that was
missing
I lacked ambition as I went
through adolescence
transitions
I didn't know which way to
go
As I was swayed to and fro
With the wind
No one had ever told me
about the diamond I
possessed within
The soft rain before the
storm was a sign for me to
get it together
But the streets was good to
me and crime became my
shelter
I kept moving in the rain
Wiping raindrops from my
face

Silly me wasn't aware that I
was walking on grace
The rain started pouring
The thunder started clapping
I was a helpless child with no
direction caught up into
rapping
It got worse by the day
I should have known that
wrath and destruction were
on the way
Then one day a petty crime
turned into gun play
My life was out of control
and there was no way for me
to stop it
I was unconscious of the
consequences because my
vision was myopic
I was in a bunch of trouble
with no way out
It was during this stage of the
journey that I learned what
manhood was all about
Coming to prison was when
my young life started over
Things became a whole lot
clearer now that my mind
was sober

I had caused so many people
emotional agony and tears
It was during my depressed
days that God told me there
would be Glory years
So I re-charted my course
toward God and the sun
began to shine
Then I embraced the attitude
that victory was mine
Faith changed my fate
While still in prison I started
to do something great
Two decades later I am in
perfect alignment with my
Maker
I'm still in the midst of the
odyssey
But today I am a better me
As I continue on toward my
destiny.

Momma You Were Right-

C. W. Fleming

I was in prison on the fourth
of November when my
mother died
I laid under the cover for
hours and cried
When the Chaplain informed
that I would not be able to go
to the funeral
I was in unspeakable pain
Then it began to rain
And I saw my mother thru
the bars of my cell in the rain
under a light
In that moment I dropped to
my knees and told her that
she was right when she told
me

You're going to get in some
trouble that I can't get you
out of
A hard head makes a soft
behind
If you'll lie- you'll steal
You're starting to get too big
for your britches
Money don't grow on trees

If you think life is easy, just
sit back and ride
Sticks and stones will break
your bones- but words will
never hurt
It's better to say there he
goes rather than there he lays
Ain't nothing in the streets
after midnight but trouble
and death
If you can dance and sing for
the devil, then you can come
to church and worship the
Lord
You are not going to stay
here and not go to school or
work
Boy you are not too big for
me to beat
I will beat you like a Hebrew
slave
I will beat you back into
yesterday
The only friend you have is
Jesus
Blood is thicker than water
I brought you into this world
and I will take you out

If you are big enough to
make the mess, you are big
enough to clean it up
I didn't raise you like that
The grass always looks
greener on the other side
The bird you have in your
hand is better than the two in
the bush
The race of life is not won by
the fastest runner- slow
down
Ain't nobody gonna put up
with your mess after I'm
gone
I would surely like to see you
change before it's too late
Son, I don't know what's
gonna happen after I'm gone.
My momma was right
Your momma was right
Don't wait until it's too late
to change and tell your
momma
"Momma- you're right."

Goodbye Mother-
C.W. Fleming

The day I watched you kill
daddy was the day I was
destined to be a
baddie
After dealing with such a
tragic event
Our mother/son
relationship was
drastically spent

Such a colossal act of
violence brought into our
lives an eerie silence
I declared the lie you
enticed me to say
Though we both knew it
didn't happen that way

That dark secret kept
coming at a high price
Prompting me to attempt
suicide twice
Unable to live
comfortable with myself
Alcohol and drugs I
indulged for help

Even they were useless in
numbing the pain of
watching you blow out
my daddy's brains

It's too difficult living
this lie anymore
Harboring this poison
since I was four
Lost is my freedom for
failure to seek treatment
Hiding what you and I
know of this terrible
secret

I'm unable to conceal
this anymore
The only way for me to
possibly be free
Is to reveal to the world
what you did to my
daddy and me
Goodbye mother
Goodbye lie
Goodbye.

My Secret- *by Hope*

There's a secret of mine I'd
like you to know
But I dare not say it for I
fear you may turn and
go.
It's about my life and is a
part of me
But when I make a new
friend then explain it to
them they tend to run
and flee.
Though this doesn't
change my personality or
cause me to hide my
social flare
Yet I'd like to know in my
heart that after knowing
you would still care.
When this secret
happened, I felt my life
had been wrecked.
Instead of feeling sorry for
myself I had a
complete self-check
It has made some of my
time hard and not so very
nice

That's when I turned to
God for His loving
advice.
In the end, all I wanted
was a true friend
Not some fake
opportunist playing
pretend.
In here and out there I
will always
Be a real man who
happens to have the virus
known as H.I.V.

Furious- *Markiet*
Loggins, Sr.
They say it's better to be
pissed off than pissed on.
No matter how you try to fix
it or explain girl you were
wrong.
We've been together ten long
years but when I got my time
you
up and disappeared.
You left me with no
explanation when I was at
my worse.
They say what's love got to
do with it?
All I know is it hurts.
Never thought that the girl
I loved
Would up andtake flight
like Noah's dove.
Leaving me disappointed,
curious and furious.
After ten long years I
thought our love was
serious.
Three kids, two cars and a
house.

Designer hand bags, Exotic
jewelry, I even put a ring on
your finger
and called you my spouse.
But you were more like a
mouse a smaller version of a
rat.
Allthe time on the low
trying to get my Stacks,
So now I don't feel bad for all
the dirt I did behind your
back.
I know you can't relate to
furious yet,
But you will when you
realize that you're just a
well-kept pet.
Thinking about you makes
me regret the day we met
But I learned my lesson and I
am no longer hot. The things
you valued were crumbs that
I forgot.
So move on. Carry on enjoy
life.
I learned the hard way
that no-one can make
someone like you a
housewife.

Thank You- *C.W. Fleming*

Thank you for continuously
loving me
And not judging and
condemning me-
For your assistance in this
spiritual fight
For receiving and standing
with my wife-
For speaking life into my son
For letting the world know
that despite what happened
We are one
Thank you for the letters,
magazines and books
For putting money on my
books
I know there's no way I can
pay you back
But know that I too will
always have your back.

Angry Now- *Peek*

In this cell I sit
With my heart in a pit
I try to smile
With my emotions in a pile
Every day I try to deal
With my anger I lose the will
I will plow on with my day
In this cold bunk I lay
I'm here on my own
Anger is my tone.

The Broken System- *C.W. Fleming*

We first met when I was
sixteen
You judged me deviant,
delinquent and mean
You sent me upstate
Where I learned that boys get
raped
That was the beginning of my
life on paper
Since then you have become
my justified hater
You judged me again three
years later
You said my response to
poverty
Didn't justify robbery
That I was a menace to
society
You sentenced me to five
years in your penitentiary
Where I slaved in the field
without being given an
opportunity
To learn how to fix cars or
build
I got out doing right trying to
keep it real

When I went looking for a
job
They thought I had come to
rob
So I sold drugs to do drugs
You locked me up again and
judged me a thug
You gave me twelve years
and put me on psychotropic
drugs
I was released addicted
My mind had constricted
Three months later I was
recommitted
When you judged me again
I wondered if there was any
way for me to win
So I took all of your classes,
programs and trades
When I got out two-hundred
dollars a week was all I could
get paid
So please help me
understand the wisdom
Of being locked up in your
broken system.

Missing Momma- *Torrick McMurray, Sr.*
The day they told me my
mother died
I layed motionless for three
days under my covers and
cried
When I was told the news- I
became depressed in that
instant
It happened in the first year
of my 45 year sentence
I know my incarceration
added to her stress
It caused her so much pain
knowing that I was in this
mess
For the next three years I was
psychologically vulnerable
Because of the neurosis
caused by not being able to
go to the funeral
Seven years have passed and
I am still very hurt
I can still hear her asking me
why did I sell dope instead of
work.

Even now when I think about
it my eyes become like a dam
about to burst
Cause like a fool I loved the
game instead of putting
momma and family first.

Time- *Charles Green*
Fifty was the time that they
gave me
And now,
I know only God can save me
Fifty years away from my
family and our life
But now,
I know Jesus has already
paid the price
Fifty years seems like an
eternity
But God's love brings me
serenity
Now I know fifty ain't
nothing but a number
It's just time.

The Wages of Sin- *C.W. Fleming & Griffen*

Sin starts off feeling good
and then it ends in pain
Sin is the reason why so
many people have gone
insane
Sin will keep you derelict,
depressed and in the dark
Sin will keep you from hitting
the mark
Sin can come in the form of
weed, alcohol or meth
Sin will always cause mental,
spiritual and financial death
Sin can cause you to be
malicious or live in excess
Sin will lead to reprimand,
rebuke and regrets
Sin can be as inconspicuous
as a black ant on a black rock
in the pitch- black midnight
Sin will always make doing
bad deeds and ill-gotten gain
feel right
Sin will lead you to the table
with murderous friends
Sin will cause you to lose
your freedom and die in the
pen
Sin's enemies are grace,
mercy and wisdom
Sins can always be forgiven
Sins will cease when they are
confessed
Sins can turn into
testimonies when you are
blessed
Sin dies when you walk
through faith's door
Take the step and then go
and sin no more.

Dear Baby Daddy

A. Jackson

I know this may come off as
cruel
But you're such a silly fool
You were out here trying to
impress strangers by driving the
flyest cars
Now you're broke and all alone
behind bars.
Talking about what you did for
our son
When you were out here all you
did was party and have fun
You bought him two outfits and
some Jordan's
So what you want me to do?
Write the Governor and ask for
a pardon for you?
No. I'm not going to write you
weekly or register my phone-
when for weeks on end you left
us home alone
I think you might want to call
Jerome, Malone or Tyrone.
But whatever you do don't try
prison hooch or dope

Oh yea, and I heard you
might not wanna drop the
soap
Don't worry about us cause we
gone be alright
I'm a real woman who will hold
the house down and teach our
son how to fight
You gone be alright you just
gotta write your so called friends
who was down with you when
you had some ends
Oh my bad-
They were playing pretend
No, you being locked up don't
make me glad
It's actually sad.
No, I'm not mad anymore.

Dear Baby Mama- *A.*
Jackson
I'm not trying to
burglarize your time or
interrupt your life
I know I have no claims
on you because you are
not my wife
But while I'm on lock I
want you to hold my son
down
And let him know that I
will hook him up when I
am free.
Let him know that he is
the most important part
of me.
Don't ever allow another
man to hit on my son
If that ever happens we
are eternally done
And what will come next
will definitely not be fun
The week before I got
busted it seemed like we
were on the verge of
getting back together

But since I've been on
lock you ain't even wrote
a letter
I only got forty months
to do
Don't wait until my
sentence is through to let
me hear from you
Write soon and send me
some flix
Keep me in your mix
Hook up the phone so I
can call
When I'm released
You, me and my son are
gonna ball.
Signed,
Baby Daddy

Queen- *C.W. Fleming*

In beauty, integrity and character

You are my Queen

A rare human being

My good thing

My sweet thing

God's finest creation

An example to generations

More celestial than the highest constellation

Deserving of all my admiration

Good to the core

A champion for the poor

Always looking to do more

The reason causing my vision to soar

Intentionally meek

A source of strength to the weak

Mind so deep

If you ever were to weep

There would be blood in the streets

Mother of a prince

Teacher of a nation

The source of my inspiration

Nurturer of seeds

Fulfiller of my every need

My soul's motivation

A CEO, entrepreneur and Skills Specialist

Our family's gold medalist

Your light shines brighter than the brightest star

Queen of my Kingdom is who you are.

Trill Kick'n- *by Carlton S.*

Listen to me
Levitate with me
Gravitate to me and lose
yourself in this divine artistry
Motivation, meditation,
mind rehabilitation
Determination to destination
through prostration
Levitation, no
procrastination or limitation
leaning in the light
Inclination through
revelation, mind motivated
to move nations from
Mis-education, self-
glorification and denying
that we are a gangsta nation
To whom the enemy deems
useless
Nullification
This is mind motivation
Gentrification of this urban
gangsta nation
From the deaf, dumb and
blind state

Emancipation, self-
proclamation, standing firm
through self-edification
Revving the mind's
resuscitation to derail the
mind of deterioration
This is detoxification of that
diabolical mind that loses all
the time and makes bad deals
and causes self and the
family but itself it never kills
Got to keep it trill
Reality
Once upon a time we were all
lost now it's back to life.
What's the use of existence if
nobody's free?
Kicking knowledge and
wisdom cause if one of us is
chained
Nobody's free
Who said I was speaking
about physically?
The mind controls all
Spirit
If it's not purified, you can
walk out the golden gates
and still not be free

From the state of mental
intoxication to the brink of
complete annihilation
You have to initiate
Your mental reformation to
arrive at spiritual
transformation

Chango- *WC McMullin*
From whence comes the
saying
"Well I'll be a monkey's
uncle?"
How for the sake of common
decency
Could such atrociousness
come to be
And how could such
ambiguity
Possibly relate to me?
Consider my evident
pedigree
My innate ability- my will to
be
Constantly striving degree by
degree
Pursuing upward mobility
Up, up and away they say
Tis dawn- a brand new day
Where unsubstantiated leaps
in DNA
Are presumed correct
without sway
And held as fact without
delay
Especially to some in every
way

And what a travesty they
portray
How did ignorance come to
rule the day
With unfounded theories as
the mainstay
When truth is so easy to
convey
Decrying a standing genetic
free-fall
Awaiting a long overdue
overhaul
Where conspiracy theories
spearhead the call
And blatantly falsehoods
chosen overall
Which I do abhor and do
appall
Cause I am no kin to a
monkey at all.

Surrender All- WC McMullin

Mr. Policeman...
How much destruction have
you wrought?
How many heartaches have
you brought?
And how many lives have you
left distraught?
How much restrain have you
with your gun?
When the defenseless child is
on the run?
Hands high! We comply!
Mr. Officer, don't off him sir!
Mr. Officer, please don't off
him sir.
Mr. Policeman...
Have you a heart?
Or is that the part of you
that's missing?
Or is that the start of your
dissing?
Mr. Policeman...what exactly
do you gain
From the pain wrought by
your disdain?
Hands high! We comply!

Mr. Officer, don't you off him
sir!
Mr. Officer, don't you off him
sir.
Mr. Policeman...
What in the world are we to
do?
When your gun has no
conscience same as you?
When recurring death is
déjà vu
When you indict and kill
those in flight
In the face of your might,
don't I have the right
To live?
Hands high! We comply!
Mr. Officer, don't off him sir!
Mr. Officer, please...don't off
him sir.

Mr. Policeman...
You've got license to kill...at
will...no bill
What a deal...and yet and
still...
You kill, you kill and again
you kill!
Mr. Officer, don't off him sir!

Just ain't no future in the
coffin sir!!

Love Will Outlast the Pain- *Kevin Burns*

If I had a magic wand I'll
tell you what I'd do
I would duplicate the
word love and summon it
would to sit next to you.
The "L" would be for
loyalty, because you have
honored our name.
The "O" we will be for
OUR continuing pain.
The "V" is for victory,
that I know we will have
over the hurt.
The "E" is for every time
we allow love and loyalty
to work.
First, I want to apologize
for being here in this
pen.
It happened because of
my disobedience to God
and my continuing sin.
The last time I saw you,
you were engulfed in
tears;
You couldn't accept my
judgment of an
aggravated 35 years.
We were immediately
separated, I thought all
hope for our family was
lost.
I cried out to God and
asked Him how could I
pay what my sin had
cost.
God told me His son had
paid when He willingly
accepted my sins on the
cross.
So I again apologize to
you for living a life of
wrong.
And I thank God that
today our family is
united and strong.
Today I want you to
know that I love you with
all of my heart;
Once I'm home I promise
you that we will never
again be apart.
You are my best friend

I thank God for you
again and again.
I also thank God for
sending His son to die
for our sins and for
instilling in our hearts
that our family will never
end.

Words I Never Told My Daddy- *Elmer J. Lockett*

I hated you man
Because you were never
around when momma's
boyfriend slapped me
around.
When you got out of
prison I wanted you to be
my daddy.
I wish you would have
But you were on the
streets crushing my
heart- filling it with hate
I didn't love you
anymore
Who could have, but
God?
After 16 years in prison,
you told me that you
were proud of me
Because of the changes
that God had made in me
At the time, you were
living only a few cells
down from me.

That's when I got to
know you were, who you
are.
And I really love you.
You filled that empty
daddy space that was in
my heart.
You taught me loyalty,
honor and to do right
even if I had to stand
alone.
I love you Pops and I
wish we could've had
more time before God
called you home.

**Holding On, Pressing
On**- *Elmer J. Lockett*
23 hours a day locked up
in my cage
With no one but myself
on which to take out my
rage
My sanity seems to be
closer to leaving than
staying
The enemy whispers to
me to give up on praying
Surrounded by hatred,
heartache,
discouragement,
depression and rejection
A spiritual, emotional
cesspool
A living pit of despair
Alive and thriving yet
there is no life there
How do I keep going?
How do I hold on when I
can't see anything worth
holding on to?
When I feel that all my
help is gone
I will pray without
ceasing

I will be the light in the
darkness
I'll hold on tight to my
faith, fighting the good
fight
Holding on.
Pressing on.

Get Up- *C.W. Fleming*
You've been convicted of a
crime- but you're not a
criminal
You were caught doing
wrong- but you're not a
wrongdoer
You've sinned as have all
men- but the race of life is
still yours to win
Get up!
You are hurting- but you
shall heal
You are alone- but you will
live
You've fallen- but you have
not failed
Get up!

Mass Incarnation- *C.W.*
Fleming

People are being locked up in
waves
Held in concrete caves
Made into modern day slaves
They lose their right to vote
The suicide statistics suggest
they also lose their hope
The vast majority are locked
up for dope
Or having lost their ability to
cope
In a society where they were
miserable
Living in poverty made them
invisible
As soon as they took a chance
to come up
They were locked up
Taxpayers pay thirty-five
thousand a year to people
who shoot deer
To keep them in a perpetual
state of fear
So, they come out worse than
when they went in
Destined to be captured as a
slave again

Nationwide they are
spending 82 billion to lock
up 2.3 million
Mostly blacks and browns
So, in America- slavery is still
around
Oops! My bad.
That's an exaggeration
They call this mass
incarceration!

Do Time- Don't Let It Do You- *C.W. Fleming*

Doing time is a test of mental
endurance
Excelling in education and
faith shows prudence
The real struggle is to guard
against evil's foolishness
Continually build family
relations
Be careful not to destroy
outside connections
Focus your energy on your
life after the House of
Corrections
In prison, it's better to have
respect than a friend
Face your fears
Stand alone and never seek
protection from men
Loving your neighbor is not
expected
The love of God is often
misunderstood and rejected
Sex with anyone will be a
mistake
The consequences will be
more than you can take

The best person to spend
time with is yourself
If you have any time left-
spend it with your other self
While in prison cure yourself
of gluttony and greed
Forgive yourself for your
misdeeds
And
Read, read, read!

The Way Forward- *C.W. Fleming*

I shall proceed in my purpose
despite prison's pugnacious
and perverse milieu
I shall never lament about
what is lost
I shall labor to love those like
me
My legacy will loom large
If I can enlighten those
locked up and left behind
I shall encourage, enthuse
and enhance
The life of my son and my
wife
Even from this enclosure my
empire shall excel
My vision for victory shall be
voiced over the vicious and
vile villains who seek to make
me a victim of this vicinity
My sight shall sail
unrestricted from the
system's ridiculously sparse,
segregated cells
To spearhead spectacular
successes in the souls of the
forgotten building blocks of
society
I shall climb to the feet of
Martin, Maya and Malcolm

By every means necessary I'll
rise again from my cage and
sing
I have a dream that will
mend the lives of the broken
men
The gruesomeness of this
living graveyard shall not
gorge my gait
With God as my guide I shall
be grand to every man-
good when I should
And great when least
expected
My journey is to the end
Into eternity
Through the Golden Gates
Into the Pearly Gates
Beyond the seventh level to
To the edge of illuminated
light
Where I will kneel and tell
Him that though I fell
I still continued to fight.

Like Father, Like Son- *Lion M. O'Neil*

They say the apple never falls too far from the tree

A splitting image like a mirror just another one of me

You can tell by the eyes they're the windows to the soul

Facial features manifested in the face as he grows

From a boy into a man journey started as a youth

As the trials and tribulations calculated into truths

Father told me who I was and even blessed me with my name

The bloodline pumped love from my heart through my veins

Learn the keys to the knowledge he departed as he left

So I would understand and use the wisdom for myself

Your actions spoke louder than the words from your tongue

So I thank you and 1 love you, to a father from his son.

You Can't Spell America Without Me-

King David Dunn

You can't spell America without me

Even though we're considered drags of society

Black, red, white, yellow or brown

Yeah- that's me

I'm from every town

I'm man, woman even a child

We come from every city, town and state

Me, a part of America you've come to hate

You find me on every highway that you rid

I'm in every town that you reside

Every step that you make

When you wash your car- that's me

The license plate

I'm even the new safety sticker issued by the state

Naw, you can't spell America without me

When your kids go to college there I'll lie

The dorm furniture, yeah that soft mattress-that's me

I'm part of the state parks that you explore

I'm that white uniform that you try to ignore

But Old Sam loves me the best

When we clean him up after the birds have left him a mess

You can't spell America without me

I'm the cheapest labor in the state you see

I'm your brother, sister, son and daughter.

Along with a husband, wife and fathers

You can't spell America without me

Even when I am finally set free

Psychological Battle-*King David Dunn*

If the pen is mightier than the sword -
Then let this cut run deep into the psyche of your sinful
mind
Cause i ts time To
pay you back
With a spiritual attack
Upon the l ies that you represent
And the way you presented yourself to me as a totally free spirit
Satan, I ' m not trying to hear i t
Or be anywhere near your psychological babble Now th at
I' ve found Jesus I can unravel the sinful
thoughts you put in my mind As I
ascribe to Psalms 29
The voice of the Lord is upon the waters that I walk on
I curse thee in my Father' s name
Get thee behind me Satan
No longer will I be entertained by you
It' s over
I' m done
I' m through
I have no fear of thee
Because Jesus' death set me free
It' s always a battle when we l ive in sin
Sometimes i t can destroy our spiritual friends
Even though they were still just a babe in Christ who tried to
bring us out of the devil' s crypt
Freewill is a double- edged sword It can
maim and destroy
Or i t can be the greatest of joy.

I' m Innocent - *C. W. Fleming*

I' ve never been arrested before. Crime is something I attest and
abhor.
The only reason I' m in this mess is because I' m poor.
I' m innocent

This isn' t funny. I don' t have any money to get a lawyer
to prove my alibi; all these charges a re a l ie.
I' m innocent.

The bond is too high for me to pay.
The judge wouldn' t l isten to nothing I had to say. They
have the wrong fingerprints and no DNA
I' m innocent.

I didn' t do i t. I wasn' t there - do you believe me?
Do you care? I'
m innocent.

Injustice will never prevail.
I' m catching hell. As
anyone can tell, I' m
innocent.

My Reality of Prison-
Willie Joe McAdams

Hot nights and hot days
A lot of work and no pay
A legalized slave of the state is correct to say
Locked in a cage with rage
Will I go crazy?
I endure dehumanization daily
It's as if they have been trained to treat me less than a man
They'll violate my constitutional rights if I complain
Their procedures and policies are developed to drive us insane
They say that the taxpayers are taking care of me
Their money would be better spent on healthcare rather than on
indefinitely holding me
While their guards continually beat on me
Steel is old and cattle are almost gone
Prison is the new way to get the rich on
Making a billion dollars off of our need to use the phone
Hiding us behind rural redneck towns
The old are dying from the Texas heat
Vendors are getting rich just by selling us junk to eat
And a decade on lock for selling rocks makes my resume weak
Statistics say I am destined to repeat
I know I did the crime and I should do my time
But is it right that they should seg me in violation of my "due
process rights"
And then threaten to beat me within an inch of my life because
one of their employees came to work not feeling right

Body cams for police was a good decision

Now they need to have body cams on guards inside of prison

Because they put us in cuffs and then beat us until we are

unconscious

Other inmates rarely speak up for their fallen peers

They won't talk about it out of fear

They themselves are just praying to safely make it out of here

I write this today because my spirit is strong

But after fourteen years all I want to do is go home

I want and need to forget all the wrongs of this prison life

I need to be healed by the love and compassion that will be in my

new life.

Ms. T. Jones- *C.W. Fleming*

I'm writing to you about your son Don

I'm sad to say he's died. He's gone.

We were always together.

He was like my big brother.

He is the one who introduced me to Faith.

Watching him live taught me that love was better than hate.

He loved you and talked about you all the time.

He was always afraid of you passing before he finished his time.

How ironic is it that he's gone

before he could make it home.

He had a heart attack and died on the spot.

He was really a good person who did a lot.

Both the guards and the gangs gave him respect.

He didn't lie, cheat, curse or make bets.

He had really changed from 23 years ago

Nobody can understand why parole wouldn't let him go.

I think that's really wrong.

But I know he is free in his new home.

They don't let us have funerals for our friends when they pass.

So I just wanted to write and tell you that Don was a man with class

Will you please tell his daughter that her father was a good man?

Please tell his grandchildren about him if you can.

He always talked about getting out and running with them.

I hope the angels will sing him hymns.

God Bless You,

-John

Mrs. T. Brown- *C.W. Fleming*

Mrs. Brown I am writing
you about your son
Sawyer.
He died unnecessarily,
and I think you need a
lawyer.
He fell off the top bunk,
hit his head on the bars
during a seizure.
He was off his
medication because
medical wasn't following
procedures.
The truth is he wouldn't
be dead,

if he had been given his
seizure meds.
He had written several
requests to be seen,
But the medical staff is
so very mean.
He had been waiting for
a long while
For the doctor to review
his file.

Last week he was
shaking, dizzy and about
to faint,
He told me his problem
and asked me to help
him file a complaint.

Now that he's dead
they'll try to brush it
under the rug.
They are indifferent to us
because they say that we
are just convicted thugs.
Even though your son
was a convicted felon,
As a veteran he had a
right to his medicine.
With seizures he
shouldn't have been on
the top bunk anyway.
His discharge date was
just eight weeks away.
Sawyer was a good dude.
He was polite and never
rude.
He read Tom Clancy and
Grisham and stayed to
himself.
He once told me that you
and his father were all he
had left.
Mrs. Brown, I am really
sorry about what
happened to Sawyer.
Please inquire about the
events leading to his
death with a lawyer.

Ms. T. Smith- *C.W. Fleming*

Ms. Smith I am writing
to tell you that your son
"Dinky" got killed last
night.
The way it went down
wasn't right.
He was found stabbed to
death in the kitchen's
vegetable vault
Whoever did it hasn't
been caught
The guards didn't like
him because he could
fight- but they didn't kill
him.
Whoever killed him was
probably someone who
was always with him.
The first rumor was that
it was the Mexicans over
a bet.
Now I'm hearing it was
violence gone bad from
his own set.
Others say it was the
wood pile and over
incoming smoke.
Then I heard it had been
done by a "loc" he had
bullied when he was
broke.
The whole hood is gonna
wanna know how did
Dinky come to an end.

As his lifelong friend I
am here to say he was a
G till the end.
If you want to talk about
it put some money on my
phone.
They will bury his body
here if you ain't got the
money to bring him
home.
Tell his baby mama that
was foul what she did,
And she knows that
Dinky always loved his
kid.
Ms. Smith I am sorry
about the way Dinky
died.
But I wanted to write to
tell you because I know
how people lie.
 – Jamaal.

Fly Free- *C.W. Fleming*

I see you in your cell. I've
felt what you feel.
It's hell. It's real.
I know you pace the
floor; watch the door and
the carvings on the wall.
I know you can't stand
the yellings, screamings
and calls.
I know you're in there
behind a lie- or
something you did
impulsively and can't
remember why.
I know you can't cry,
and that you've thought
it might be better if you
die.
I know you've looked at
the ceiling and thought
about ways to end your
feelings.

Let me show you how to
free yourself from the
funk
Lay back on your bunk
And just be still.

Close your eyes and don't
feel what you feel.
Breathe, breathe,
breathe.
Now look inside your
mind.
Take your time.
Listen inside your mind.
Take your time, turning
your eyes inside.
Open them and look
down inside of you.
Travel down inside of
you until you find-
the original you.
Look at the people who
love you.
Remember the gifts God
gave you.
Breathe, breathe,
breathe.
Avoid the hell of your cell
by diving deeper into
you.
Remember the love,
laughs and fun.
Now forgive yourself for
what you've never done.

I know you feel like a
mess.
But this is a time you
must talk to yourself.
Softly say, "I forgive me."

Be free.
Be free, now allow your
imagination to show you
your destiny.
With your eyes closed see
your arms turning into
wings.
Fly into the future and
see new things.
See your new life. Laugh
with your new friends.
Your imagination is
limitless and it never
ends.
Look at where you will be
after year three.
Fly into year ten.
You are bound to win.
Did you know the
Kingdom of God is
within?
Peace is also within.

You can lay there and fly
free within until it all
ends.
If you stay inside of you,
you can deal with
whatever is outside of
you.

I declare and decree that
you shall live and not
die-
And here's why.
God knows the plans He
has for you.
They are for you to live
and laugh.
Remember that this day,
moment and time shall
pass.
Read this again and fly
free.
Again and again and
again.

A Day in Prison- *C.W. Fleming*

It begins with the
clanging sound of steel
doors shutting.
Followed by the sniffles,
sneezes and sadness of
the sick.
The inmates and guards
all look mean-spirited,
merciless and mad.
The breakfast of watery
grits, thinned out
powdered milk and
flour-deficient cold
pancakes sets the
morning mood of
extreme melancholy.
The unprovoked yelling
of insensitive newly
hired guards will bash
the best of hopes of a
better day.

By noon, inmates and
guards are becoming
neurotic.
The mundaness of slave
jobs makes you feel
idiotic.

Lunch is always a
letdown.
Lost in the world of
lunacy makes you begin
to feel less than left
behind.
Public showers are
humiliating.
Negative thoughts are
always formulating.
If it's summer the heat
can be more than a
bummer-
it can be a killer.
In your cell after work
you only have a flat
mattress with no pillow.
Evil engrosses the
environment by evening.
Empathy is absent as
anxiety appears to be all
around.
The evening meal is the
worse.
Pork and beans, fried
rice or casserole, most
likely served unseasoned
and cold.

Without commissary
many inmates will feign
A second helping of pork
and beans.
At night, the TV is the
drug.
It keeps the population
numb as they vie over
sports shows and re-
runs.
The phone is the straight
shot home.
That is if you have
anybody at home.
After mail call,
everybody is acting like
they ain't alone.
It will be only seconds
before something goes
down.

Contraband drugs and
smoke is all over the
place.
Danger, desperateness
and despair is now in the
air.
Perverted erotic lust
begins to be spewed.

Secret lovers are coming
unglued.
The fights are fast but
seldom fierce.
A lot of thugs are trying
to get tatted and pierced.
The gambling is intense.
Who will get paid keeps
us all in suspense.
At 10:30 pm it all ends.
You survived another day
and so you win.
Now you go into a cell
with a stranger who's
strange.
On the way to sleep you
feel the loneliness which
is prison's worst pain.
You try to have the joy of
a private memory of a
loved one or good sex.
You whisper a silent
prayer and refuse
yourself a cry.
The next morning it
starts again as the doors
start to clang and bang.

Nothingism- *C.W. Fleming*

Nothingism is playing dominoes with strange foes.

Lying about how you slammed Cadillac doors- was never poor.

After doing it all day, you wake up to do it some more.

Nothingism is to memorize Jordan, Kobe and Lebron's stats,

Then spend all day arguing about football, basketball and bats.

While your skin is flaking from tats,

not caring that your family has not food in the vats.

Nothingism is to debate how far Heaven is from the black hole;

or that Hell is at the farthest point of the South Pole.

Nothingism is to spend twenty years in the penitentiary and

never get a G.E.D. – while arguing that a man's sexual preference

can be determined by the way that you pee.

Nothingism is chasing cigarettes, drinking hooch or smoking

"tu-tu," and playfully running around grabbing another man's

"too-too."

Nothingism is denying God.

Faking like you're hard.

Bumping back with the guards and never sending your kids a

card.

Nothingism is deplorable.

It'll leave you empty, uneducated and unemployable.

Nothingism is to be in prison without goals, a dream or a vision.

Nothingism is the primary cause for institutionalization.

Avoid it at all costs to maximize your rehabilitation.

Nothingism will camouflage itself as a time filler;

But in reality it is a silent and slow cognitive killer.

Today, replace Nothingism with reality acceptance-

And stop being complacent

while enduring this temporary displacement.

Christmas on Lock- *C.W. Fleming*

On Christmas morning when I saw the men come off the block
I thought it was the saddest day on lock.
Their faces were lethargic, leathery and long
It made me wonder if they were ever going home.
Eating a special meal was the only agreed upon tradition
The story of Jesus' birth got no special attention.
There were no Christmas trees, mistletoes or singing "Bells Will
Be Ringing."

So I read to them the story of the Savior's birth
However, they still looked hopeless, helpless and hurt.

Not even the promise of a free gift gave their broken spirits a life.
So I asked them all what did Christmas mean to them;
They recited one word together as if it was a hymn
FAMILY.
How could I have forgotten all the family members on lock?
Too many have been forgot-
Next Christmas, let's bring the family to the forgotten ones on
lock.

Passion

"Passion will move men beyond themselves, beyond their shortcomings and beyond their failures." – Joseph Campbell

Passion- *Kielyn Reed*

I would've froze from the bitter cold when I was cast into the
bottomless hole of life without parole had it not been for passion.

I was given a life sentence when I was a teenaged menace.
It was a bid I never would have finished if it weren't for passion.

I was innocent of the accused crime. My people didn't have a dime.
The false incarceration occurred during my sexual prime. At times I
wanted to die doing that time and I would have if not for passion.

The drive and hope of it keeps us overly enthusiastic- regardless of
the depressing facts of our reality. It's the candle that continuously
burns in the darkest chamber of our hearts.
It wakes us and makes us exquisitively sensitive about the
importance of spiritual, emotional and sexual intimacy. Despite our
felonious incarceration, passion still drives us to experience the joy,
pain and sorrows that are only possible with family and very personal
human connections.

When the dehumanization, humiliation and hopelessness of
incarceration ambushes our determination- it's passion that pushes
us to keep on pushing.

A grown man sits staring aimlessly at the concrete wall.
He's lost his mother and his passion rises and falls.
An older man's ardent desire was to once again see his wife's face.
Now that she's died he will surrender to this place.

A hardened convict who hadn't seen his daughter in years, got a picture of his new grandbaby and cried crocodile tears.

It's the inevitable propelling power of passion that impels the immobile to continue to move through the madness of another mundane day when their parole has for the tenth time been turned away.

Daily we surge ahead through utterly dark circumstances with the quintessential hope of a second chance.

It's what drives the man who has never had the opportunity to experience romance. He was locked up at 16, then a Latin king.

He stayed true to his crew.

Now at forty-two he has no idea what a woman's love can do.

So he eagerly waits to see if all he's heard of love is true.

He's thirty –three and he cries relentlessly about how his dying mother and special needs brother needs him free.

He's sixty-two and during his dreams, he reaches into space for someone who is not there. Yet he faiths forward through year 42 of his incarceration believing that someday someone will be there to hug him before he dies.

His time is excruciatingly hard.

He's isolated in seg for 23 hours a day for hurting a guard.

His passion is for God.

All night long he prays passionately to see his Lord.

So come into the lion's den and experience the vastness of the pride.

You'll be tantalized and thrilled by the passions you find inside.

We also hope you'll understand that our passion to be home with you has never died.

The Journey to the First Time- *C.W. Fleming*

At first you were my friend
Our early morning embraces
pulled me in
Your smile turned my smile
into a to grin
Then you gave me that note
that said to pencil you in
That was when I first started
to desire a taste of your
caramel-candied skin.
When I sat in my office and
read your note, I laughed and
chuckled until I almost
choked
I thought you to be real, rare
and pure; but too young for
sure.
Oh how wrong I was and very
shortly thereafter our
relationship was a buzz
That day we went to the park
and walked and talked
I found you to be fascinating,
intriguing and without a fault
When you began to bring me
breakfast on my second job
was about the time my heart
began to throb
You were sweet and kind and
I was my own man with my
own mind
I was smooth but my life was
complex 'cause I had hidden
lovers and an ex
To me it was a mystery how
slowly, yet methodically you
were winning me
Then without prompting I
professed you to be my
future wife and my destiny
Then came the heart attack
You never left my side- you
had my back
Then here was the day that I
had you so hot that we both
knew you were ready to pop
But with love and out of
respect I brought everything
to a stop
Then our first time finally
arrived and it was all the way
live
As our bodies began merging
I realized that you really were
a 7-year virgin.

A Poem of Love- *Oscar Stephen III*

Living a life with drama and pain

Hoping and praying that I don't go insane

Told to do right but all I did was wrong

I was also told that I wouldn't live this long

Suffered two times from aneurisms in the heart

Satan tried to kill me and take me apart

Revived on the operating table and brought back to life

In the back of my mind I knew it was Christ

This is my testimony I had to tell

Cause since I gave my life to Christ everything the devil has tried has failed

So this poem of love was created to help, encourage and bless

In the bosom of Christ the heavy laden can find rest

To all my brothers and sisters who are doing time with me-

Be Blessed!

Angel That Flew Too Close to the Ground - S. Hall

Though my life turned
out lonely, at one time it
was great
Love was all around me-
free from the turmoil and
hate.
Looking back now at all
the regrets that I have
If only I'd done it
differently, I would not
be so sad.
But there is one who
stands beside me no
matter what.
He's willing to accept all
of the shortcomings that
I got.
Early on, I was one of
His chosen angels to be.
But then it happened and
the devil said hello to me.
In a downward spiral no
bottom in sight,
I struggled, kicked and
screamed with all my
might.
Then the day happened
rock-bottom I have hit.
That terrible day
happened and this lonely
prison cell is where I sit.
So I sit here and ponder
the what-if and could've
beens.
I chose the road less
traveled and said
goodbye to all my
friends.
Bound by Satan locked in
his cage I tried to do
good despite all the rage.
From this day forward by
Satan I will no longer be
bound.
For I will always
remember the day that I
forgot and flew too close
to the ground.

I Refuse to Believe the Lie-
Reginald Hicks, Sr.

Some people say a
"prison marriage" is
destined to fail,
Yet 50% of free-world
marriages are a living
hell.
Sure you have your
statistics, but can't tell.
...I refuse to believe the
lie!
I admit, it's tough- I have
shed some tear;
Every time I get a set off
it brings a new set of
fears;
From both my family and
friends I get the jeers.
...I refuse to believe the
lie!
I just makes no damn
sense to me;
How you say a razor wire
fence could be a bad
omen for our destiny
...I refuse to believe the
lie!

I don't care what your
statistics say!
Our marriage, our love is
here to stay,
And truth be told at the
end of the day -
Our fate is not up to you
anyway!
...I refuse to believe the
lie!
If you think I'm angry
you're damn right!
No time to relax I am
ready to fight!
Get ready- I'm coming
with all my might!
... I refuse to believe the
lie!
I am sorry forgive me I
know it's not about you.
I'm in the fight of my life
for me and my boo;
My energy and focus will
bring us through.
... I refuse to believe the
lie!

So call us " one percenters" I am good with that,
Thirteen years later my wife still have my back!
I'm still totally committed to her and that the fact!
... I refuse to believe the lie!

Second Look-

Henry Molina

Isolated but not forgotten in my situations,
In a struggle for freedom but faced with many limitations,

Been fighting against becoming institutionalized for over 20 years,
Tried defiance, tried bucking the system - but I switch gears.

I became mature in spite of the pain and loss,
I grew up in an environment were having integrity came at a high cost.

Still in high school when I was snatched into the system,

Homecoming, first job,
barely learned to drive-
so am I too a victim?

Not claiming to have
been perfect without
fault or any blame,
But I never comprehend
how my actions could
leave an everlasting
stain.

I came in a child with no
hope, no purpose, no
direction -
To having a GED,
vocational training and a
college education.
I found God, or rather
He found me is a more
accurate description,

All these amazing people
advocating for Second
Look makes hope more
than fiction.

Answer me this and I'll
end these words
searching for empathy,
Are you the same person
now that you were 17?

Can 60 years at 17 be
labeled "closing in the
book?"
Seeing who I am now,
the man I've become
deserves a second look.

Don't Throw Me Away- *Henry Molina*

Don't throw me away I
can still contribute to
society,
Give me a chance to give
back and pour into my
community,
I've changed into a man
of great responsibility,
I can raise a family,
hold a job and pay taxes
if given the opportunity,
I came in an adolescent
with no understanding of
long-term consequences,
I was thinking of the
party that weekend- not
razor wire fences,
I think back to the day
when my entire life with
rearranged,
I try to make sense of the
mistakes I made but also
realize that I've changed,
My thinking is different
on now, how I view a
value life
As a kid we make so
many bad decisions often
involving drugs, guns,
girls or a knife,
Contemplating and
calculating all the time I
lost,
Late teens, all twenties,
thirties, rolling into my
forties that was the cost,
Wading through mental
and physical penal
corridors of destruction,
I hung onto my morals,
values and my desire for
positive reconstruction,
So I ask you out there-
how much more time do
I owe you?
You society- don't throw
me away I am of great
value.

Think About It-
Henry Molina

We are so quick to slam the gavel down with a lengthy prison
term,
But what about a young person facing difficulties in life with
much to learn?
I'm not trying to come up with excuses and rationalizations.
Just speaking on immaturities, conflict resolution skills and
cognitive qualifications.
You see, I was there and I know how confusing it had been,
But I'm not him anymore, that confused child at the age of 17.
I grew up, matured and around 23 my thinking crystallized,
The ramifications of my actions were deeper than I ever realized.
But now I see so many young human beings shouting for a
second look,
Give us a chance and talk to us now about the positive road
we've took.
Give me a chance, I will not come back,
I have a life to pursue, go to work, raise a family
Do a lot of things like you.
Is it all in vain, the money we spend on educating the
incarcerated masses?
Is it just to sound good in their point just to sound good, is there
a point or is it just madness?
Statistics show I will not come back after 20 years,
I've matured into a man of aspiration,

Grace Changed Everything- *Reginald Hicks. Sr.*

Who am I and why am I here?

I've wrestled with these questions year after year;

My heart so hardened- couldn't even shed a tear!

...Grace changed everything!

Racism was something I held strong to;

Fighting and violence was what I loved to do ;

Flourishing in this culture is what got me through!

...His grace changed everything!

Waking up in segregation is a as low as it can get,

Wearing the prison stigma of a "security threat"

Like a wild animal in need of a vet!

...His grace changed everything!

In a cramped 6X9 cell I fell to my knees,

I surrendered to God and asked him please,

Allow me to go to school I'll make A's and B's!

...His grace changed everything!

I warn you now, all we confess;

Our father God will put to the test-

Ten years later and it is still a love fest

... His grace changed everything!

Grace is a gift we could never earn.

The more I experience it the more I learn,

It is a consuming fire with a slow burn!

...God's grace changes everything!

God you are faithful, that's why I sing!

Your grace is greater than all I can bring!

... God, your grace...changed everything!

A Call for Humanity-

Henry Molina

If we come together can we make a change?
A huge difference like The Second Look bill, something within
that range,
I think society finally sees that you can't throw away the key.
If you don't do it to whales, elephants are dogs- you can't do it to
human beings.
Now I'm not knocking and advocating for what is in one's heart,
I'm just saying I'm a human who has made mistakes asking for
another start.
I'm asking for a real chance at life as a man and not a child,
Let me be there for my family to get them off welfare to put it
mild.
You see my three sons need me there to help with my wife's
needs.
It's not just about me- it's about my marriage and her three
mouths she feeds.
Empathy, understanding, to place yourself in their spot -
Isn't that what humanity is?
At least that's what I thought.
I made one mistake; I gave you two decades. Just ponder that a
second.
Not minimizing what happened, only asking you to imagine.
I sit here ready to go like a horse at the gate;
Let me pay bills, minister to youth, save them because I can
relate.
We can make a change by pushing through proper legislation.
Help me to help others-
Let's come together for humanity is reformation.

Behold the Beauty of the Day- *Myron Lovings*

As I behold the beauty of the
day
I visualize a smile upon your
face
Not a day goes by that I don't
behold your beauty
So I ask myself, what has
your love done to me?
I 'm caught in your web
There's no escape
I surrender to thee
Our love is truly strong
It's allowed us to behold each
other for this long
Separated by distance and
left with only beloved
memories
My mind twisted and my
heart was lonely
All the signs said that you
were my one and only
The beauty of the feeling that
I have this day
Leaves me with only one
thing to say
Lisa- I love you as I behold
your beauty every day.

Prisoners- *C.W. Fleming*

Yes, you are a prisoner
behind steel bars.
The detainees in Gitmo are
prisoners of war.
There are millions who are
prisoners of cancer;
Whose medical condition has
no answer.
There was a boy imprisoned
for ten years in a bubble.
He died there without ever
being cuddled.
There are the imprisoned
children of Aleppo , and the
barbaric prisons of Mexico.
Yes, your imprisonment to
you is a crisis;
But it is far less problematic
than being held by I.S.I.S.
On the streets millions are
imprisoned by addictions
and millions more by
impoverished conditions.
Unlike many, our
imprisonment was caused by
our decisions to do crime.
So please- shut the heck up
and do your time!

Just My Imagination-
C.W. Fleming

Last night we had the
sweetest celebration
Deep in the depths of my
imagination
We went everywhere and did
everything
I even bought you an eight
karat diamond ring
We laughed, loved and
danced
It was a night of
unforgettable romance
We had so much fun in the
midst of love
You said you wanted to have
my son
In your eyes I saw joy, love
and hope
Until some mystical force
shook my boat
Then -
I awoke in a state of
aggravation
Realizing-
It was just my imagination
But knowing that everything
will come true
In just a little while

E-Love- *C.W. Fleming*

I was tired of a lying rap
So I got myself a dating app
After a month on E-Harmony
I went on a date that was
cool...but corny
My date was more shy than I
I wondered why but I didn't
pry
She was smart with a job and
easy on the eyes
But most importantly there
were no lies
Our second date had to be
fate
We bungee jumped and not
only was it fun
But it took away my fear of
being dumped
I can't remember when we
started holding hands
And kissing
Or all of the fun things that
we did
But all of a sudden our
relationship was serious
And the thought of not being
together made me delirious

In New Orleans we rode in a
horse pulled carriage
When we got out- I dropped
to my knee
And proposed marriage
Ten years have passed and
our marriage has been
everything I ever dreamed of
So
I am definitely a believer in
E-Love.

Let's Dance – *Joseph*
Torrey
One track
Mind in our feet
Dictating the movement
Just follow my lead
Fall back- I gotch'a
Step by step
Dipping like salsa
I'm one to take charge
But it takes two to tango
So let's allow our chemistry
To cut a rug
And sweat out our Sunday's
Best
Seven twenty spin umbrellas
Your dress
My hand on your lower back
Your hand on my chest
Slow dance position
Got our souls seeing
Eye to eye
Rain dancing to the beat of
Thunder
Something I gotta try

Let's Go Back- *Joseph Torrey*

Let's go back
To the tar paper shack
Forty-fives
Eight track
Ham bone where ya' been
Around the world and back again
School night curfew before ten
By twelve on the weekend
Except for skating rink lock-ins
Ice cream from fresh snow
Firewood from next door
Hide and seek
Freeze tag
Sleepover pallets on the floor
Cassettes dubbed VHS
Soul train
Woodstock
Peace signs on tie-dye shirts
Outside parties on the block
Foot race in the street
Double-dutch and two square
Catching lighting bugs in summer
Kool-Aid in Mason jars
Peppermint sticks in pickles
Love notes passed in class
Teacher's pets
School daze
Let's go back and make it last

Can I Fly- *Joseph Torrey*

Let me fly like a bird
With a world-wide wing span
It don't matter what kind
I'd be fly as they come
Floating to and from
Swimming in clouds
Basking in the sun
Defying gravity in whatever
locality
Uplift me
Don't shoot me down or be
mad at me
When you see me sky high
Are you sore
Because I soar
And flock together
With birds of a feather
Can I fly beyond planes
Plateaus
Expectations
With the bird's eye view
Past all stagnation
Can I glide with pride
Like an eagle or a hawk
And symbolize what doves do
Peace and love too

Amour- *Joseph Torrey*

Unique like summer rain in
the sun
The heartwarming
compassion that I have for
you makes my eyes
Misty
So I know you're the one...
 I won!
I walk with you through the
storms
Just to get to the rainbow
And absorb your struggles on
the way
Just so you can let the pain
go
I can't wait to feel you
Shield you
Conceal you
In my embrace
Undress you
Caress you
Kiss every feature on your
face
Allow nothing to come
between us
But opportunity and space

Your' a catch
I'm a chase
Our amour won't be replaced

Gestures- *Joseph Torrey*
Should've left well enough
alone
When we had the chance to
Look at what foreplay in the
doorway
Advanced to
Our minds not controlling
What our hands do
Eyes exposing each other's
desires
Pupils blazing fire
Under one another's tutelage
Guilty pleasures
Sought out
Through drastic measures ...
More than a part of me
You're the heart of me
I bleed for you
Let my body language
Express my need for you
Or should I say greed for you
Whatever it is
Too much ain't enough
You are what rhymes with
my world
My pearl
My girl
Etcetera, etcetera...

Ebony Queens- *Joseph*
Torrey

From the Nile in Nubia
To the banks of Mississippi
Black Queens
Raised nations
Warriors
Generations
Awareness
Wives of Pharaohs
Exercised influence
Over husbands
And played major roles
In political life
Before Michelle
Even after Africa
Daughters of Nefertiti
Live on
You may notice her chocolate
sway
So kinky and natural
And thick
Her hair and lips
And her skin fragrance
resembles
The dew of gods
With ointment and myrrh
Temples of Ebony Queens
Too much for the weak

To handle
All land created to be placed
Under Black Queens' sandals
For sacrifices she made for
mankind
Pay homage
Through actions of love and
loyalty
Preserve her royalty
Her highness
Add to perfection
Make her equivalent to no
minus
Appreciate her beauty
Put life on the line for it
And what makes it hard for
everyone to ignore it
Restore it

Fine Wine *by Kielyn Reed*

Can you define the way I feel without looking up my emotions?

Would you denounce the way I think if you knew it would cause a commotion?

Due to my lack of freedom I am forced to bare the pain of separation.

But they say "separation brings appreciation."

Since our separation, I have learned to appreciate those that come into my life to stay,

Like fine wine isolated in a basement for a long time-

I knew I would be opened up one day

Since you've been away I can't lie and say I have not cried-

Believe it or not, I also died inside with no way to confide.

Now my tears no longer run down my face like wasted wine-

Like Boyz II Men said in their song, *I'm Doing Just Fine.*

In the mist of my separation in this valley of pain-

I found a way to ease my pain by blocking you out of my brain.

I no longer need you or the empty promises you tried to feed me.

Like that old gospel song goes, "I was once was blind but now I see."

Now I'm a new man with my heart in my hand seeing things aft so clear.

Love is empowered by joy but pain is motivated by fear.

Drink this wine, it's been locked away since 1993-

Aged by a broken heart and soaking in these pits of misery.

Yes, soon this fine wine will be released for the entire world to taste-

But for the sins of the
women of my past out of
their glasses this wine will
waste.
Only then will they
realize, you should never
let something good go
away-
Just like fine wine it can
satisfy you in the midst of
everyday.
So for those that never
got to taste this fine
wine that has been put
on hold-

Empty out your glass
for this is a taste test
that's guaranteed to
touch the depths of
your soul.

Immortality - *WC McMullin*

Perchance to perish-all hail the death Knell-

Hoping with uncertainty that all remains well,

Expecting without a doubt, a sudden demise,

Concerned for the outcome-unable to surmise

Results and the impact of annihilation

Expiration

Dissipation

Disintegration

When threatened with perpetual extermination-

Hanging on by a bare thread, feigning survival,

Facing the untimely end-dead on arrival,

Being hopeful with the utmost vigor and vim,

Safeguarded by only an imaginary scrim;

Elimination

Liquidation

Obliteration

When there's never a good time to fade-to expire

Especially when longevity is a haunting desire.

Relinquish the frazzle-no need to toll the bell

Poetic expression subsists-it's alive and well.

Wifey- *Joseph Torrey*

Better half of me
You give me all of you
So till death do us part
I'm at the beck and call of
you
For the times you stressed
By the phone
At home alone
That's why I am spoiling you
By better half...
For the prison visits
To the county jail
I commend you
For the simple fact that
You always had my back
At the same time
All those
Other chicks
Pretend to
I intend to
Acknowledge
What you've been through
Respect has been due

Complete With You-
Elmer J. Lockett

More than words can say
More than the best
actors can convey
More than any author
could write i f he had a
series with 100 parts - is the
thanks that I give to God for
blessing me
with you
A good Christian
woman
The desire of my heart You
are truly one of a kind
You' re faithful,
committed, dedicated and
supportive through
good and bad times
Because you've loved me;
I have learned to
love
Because you believe in me;
I keep striving to succeed

Because of your walk with
me and beside me hand in
hand; I am a better man

With you as the love of
my life- my other half; I
have learned
responsibility,
accountability and I am now
a complete man

Kiss Me Them- *Willie Fleming*

Kiss me as I descend unhinged into a dismal, abysmal, abyss, where the voices of the forgotten cry out.

"THERE IS NO BOTTOM."

The smell of the rising mist" musk is the stench of burnt human hopes.

Kiss me knowing I was conceived by stars in the act of porn.

Unwanted when born,

abused for a dozen years on a farm.

Silenced with *"Kettle Corn Whiskey."*

Treated with Grand Theft Auto when frisky.

Prostituted for oxycontin, beaten for getting sick and coughing.

Trafficked as terrific at thirteen,

Killed a trick who sodomized me at seventeen, sentenced to life without parole at nineteen.

Kiss me now for real before I die in this dreadful dystopia whose

dreg is filled with fifty thousand heads of *"America's Invisible Living Dead."*

We're the poorest of the poor.

Deemed as teens unable to be cured for future use because we might return to the roost where we first suffered abuse.

Kiss me quickly while I still believe in humanity before I morph into an animal and lose my sanity like the others who must fall aimlessly for seven decades.

Whose memories fade as they wade in the nebula of the abyss crying that they can't even remember a kiss. For real!!!

Kiss me them, not with hubris but with hope for the bulk of us.

Kiss me them, for me as if you are the hero of humanity. Knowing that your lone kiss will never reach me but may save them from dying before ever experiencing an unadulterated kiss.

Father, mother it's not too late to kiss me.

Kiss me them, the orphan, immigrant, homeless, special needs, often neglected socially rejected unclean, unkept, living under the shadows in pain and shame children.

Kiss me them, father, mother, sister, brother teacher, preacher, scientist, doctor, C.E.O., magician, politician, patriot, puritan.

Kiss me them again and again.

On my forehead, eyes cheeks, ears, and noses.

Kiss away their fears and tears as I descend deeper into the bowels of the bottomless.

Into the ranks of "America's Invisible Living Dead".

They are in the shelter, in the park, in the apartment alone, under the bridge, in the cold, in the rain always sad and always in pain. Kiss them, Kiss Me, Kiss me them.

Please...Kiss me them.

I Forgave You-- C.W. Fleming

In our early years together I
was always depressed and
sad
You were a diabolical
demon who treated me
gruesomely bad
But I forgave you
You beat me, cut me,
enslaved me, deprived me
and took my children from
me
But I forgave you
You cared nothing about my
heart or my hurt
Your sole concern was my
ability to work
But I forgave you
When you were forced to let
me go- you gave me nothing
Then you got mad when on
my own I became
something
But I forgave you
You raped me with your
perverted and twisted lust
You intentionally gave me
syphilis
Yet again, I forgave you
You let loose your dogs on
my kids
You even blew up a church
that was full of my kids
And as hard as that was, I
forgave you
Right now you owe me land,
money and mules
Instead of paying me you
keep changing the rules
Playing me like I am your
forever fool
I forgive you this last time
because I am at the end of
my time
But you need to know that
the new generation
Is not the forgiving kind

Purpose

"As far as we can discern, the sole purpose of human existence is to kindle a light in the darkness of mere being." – Carl Jung

Purpose- *Kielyn Reed*

If you fail to invest then you will fail to exist.
I am yet to succeed due to the chains around my wrist.
Here we sit, wasted human potential.
Many of us are regarded as trash
Due to our indifference to our circumstances of the past
Or because of the mistakes we made when our minds were slaves to
the narcotics they gave.

It's sad, but many of us had no sense of direction.
We were never strengthened with family affections nor covered with
adequate legal protections when we entered the house of corrections.
Simply put- we had no purpose!
I fell into a hole to find my soul.
Swallowed my pride to stay alive.
Imagine falling into the deepest hole you've ever been in.
It's dark and desolate. No sign of family or friends.
In every direction you turn you see nothing but dark dirt.
Every time you close your eyes all you see are the people you hurt.
Many have forgotten how to laugh.
Others have put on an artificial mask to
mask who they were in the past
While some lose their true selves doing institutional minstrel tasks.

Head held high in the midst of so many who are still wondering why
They spent their whole lives trapped, twisted and afraid to try.
I want to have a win before I die! I want to have helped society before
my soul heads beyond the last sky.

We the incarcerated, intelligent and invisible are here to insert
purpose for future generations.
When a child has no purpose arrested development will occur over
time
For man is mind
An aimless mind will one day be doing time
Mass incarceration is not an accident and it continues to exist in the
face of declining crime.
Here's a message to the 2.3 million in the U.S. Penal system and the
ten millions world wide-
Wake up sleeping giants!
For when you do you change the tide.
Purpose or perish...
Nothing ventured, nothing gained.
WAKE UP and find your purpose and your world will change.
This world will change.
United we will change
With purpose!

Why We Write II- *C.W. Fleming*

We write to heal, to feel, to see; as therapy.

As a way to become temporarily free.

We write to experience the things we will never explore.

We write to live beyond these barbed wire fences and caged doors.

We write what we have seen when we discovered our imaginations

had wings.

We write about the tyranny of kings and the compassion of queens.

We write to right our wrongs.

To show you that thru the passage of time we've grown and that the

memory of our time together is our daily love song.

We write books, poems, letters and journals.

Some are about love and death others are spiritual and formal.

We write to remind you that even though our names are no longer

mentioned.

We are trying to make it home to you on the road of redemption.

We write to thank you for visits, prayers and support.

We ask you to ponder if mass incarceration works and to affirm

that

it is an excruciatingly painful hurt.

We write because although our punishment was banishment we are

still a part of this country, state, city and community that we love.

We write to give voice to the remorse, regrets, pain , hopes, goals,

solutions and visions that fill our mind and to have our words inked

into literary immortality if we die before finishing our time.

We write because we are still in love with you and whether you forgive us

or not; know that we are always hoping the best for you.

We write because we have something to say!!!

Change- *C.W. Fleming*

Like the caterpillar into a
butterfly
From being on your belly to
being able to fly
From being angry, violent and
delirious
Into a servant, savior and
someone serious
From being a problem that
causes social pollution
into an Urban Specialist with a
solution
Change
From taking pills, trying to steal
and running from what is real
Into a decisive, deliberate leader
with a strong will
Change
From small-mindedness, foul
language and foolishness
Into an entrepreneur with
multiple businesses
Change
From a life of carnality,
cowardliness and sin
Into a treasure and pleasure for
all men
Change

From the inside out and let it
begin with your mouth
Change
From bad to good- then help
save one person from the hood
Change
From being Godless to being
Godly
And especially from the way you
destroy your body
Change
And finally, change and become
a help to your family
Change so that you can have
gain and avoid future pain.
Change is now!

Redemption- *Antong Lucky*

Searching through this thing
called life
Looking for this thing called
right
Stumbling and fumbling over
this thing called wrong
Hoping and praying out of the
belly of darkness for the lights of
the universe to turn on
For it is when we bond our
trivialities with our purpose we
begin the descent from being
alone
Our blessings are masked as our
problems
But a deeper sense of innate
divine equips us with the
necessary tools to solve them
Never fret about the
embarrassment of falling from
grace
Because the ultimate Redeemer
worthy of praise
Has stepped in
Assumed the promise
And taken your place
Redemption.

Lady Liberty- *Rico*

Lady Liberty, sometimes I
wonder are you still here with
me.
I committed felonies and seem
to have lost my liberty.
In here it's not cool to be a
Patriot unless you're Brady.
I tend to lose when I try to
defend The Lady.
They call me crazy.
Say that I fought for the White
man. I look at social inequality
and think maybe they're right-
but maybe they're wrong.
I still remember standing on the
front line in defense of my
home.
Saw the world for what it is, so I
believe in you.
I'm only in prison because I
mistreated you; although it was
my PTSD that drove me to
become a criminal.
That's not an excuse, it's just the
truth. I understand that if
there's no justice there's no you.
I'll still fight and die for the red,
white and blue.

***Better Me*-** *Clinton T. Berry*

Trying to create a better me
so I can be a better me
Greater is He that is in
me than He that is in the
world.
So I must practice
patience and humility and
pray that I keep my sanity
When i t rains i t pours
but God can open up
all doors
Faith as little as a
mustard seed
Has me believing I can
succeed.
Faith gives me
confidence despite my
predicament
I'm not wasting time
spinning wheels
Instead
I' m s etting goals and
forming n ew
ideas
They will not only
benefit me but also
others

Yes, I'm talking about
you my brothers
My friend I' m talking
from within
As I talk with this pen Wh
at c om es f r om my m ou
th c om es f r om my heart.
Remember the message
from the start Greater is He
that is in me
All I' m doing is trying to
be a better me.

Deac- C.W. Fleming

Master disciple, community developer, decisive discerner

One-hundred-yard dash runner

Always the learner

Laboring tirelessly to help the weak become firmer

A true friend during my time of needs

Your legacy is sealed in your biological and spiritual seeds

Who is there that can count all of your good deeds?

Your gifts are many

To the poor you've given plenty

To William, Candace and I – you've been more than friendly

You make sure the brothers in seg are spiritually fed

You've expanded the flock by baptizing brothers on lock

You sing to us about "This Little Light of Mine"

And then tell us to never return to a life of crime

So don't ever forget that because of that little light of yours

This lion still roars!

A lot of love will cure a lack of love!

Always in your service,

-Flem

Uncle Willie- *Clinton T. Berry*

Mr. Willie you did i t again
You've been kind and meek
since we began.
I remember the day you
moved in
Not realizing you would be my
mentor once you settled in
It was beyond my
expectation that you would
extend your hand and show
appreciation.
Really I should have been the
one saying thank you For the
small and big
things that you do
You encourage me when I'
m down
That's why I seek your
company when I'm around I
like your advice when
you' re right and I'm wrong
Your preaching to me
helps me focus on goin g
home
You enlighten me with the best
of your jewels
I take heed c ause I' m no
fool
I can imagine the blessings you
bestow on your own
child
Wish I would have had that
maybe I wouldn't have gone
afoul.
You' re a friend I never
had
You display traits that
make me wish you were my
dad
Mr. Willie thank you for being
my friend
When I'm free it won't end.

Climate Change –
C.W. Fleming

My Son,
What's going on is extremely
alarming
It's the beginning of
Global Warming
Some countries are not heeding
the warning
Some people don't believe it will
destroy their farming
There is a hole in the ozone that
is allowing in massive ultra
violet sun rays
This is what a global group of
scientists say
Throughout the Earth, there will
be increased flooding
Fires
Hurricanes
And typhoons
Unless we all decide to act soon
The whole Earth as we know it
is doomed
The culprits are carbon, coal
and fossil fuels
The solution is to invest trillions
of dollars into energy renewal
While they argue about what
countries should pay
The glaciers are rapidly melting
away
For world leaders it's a
politically correct conversation
Yet none of them are doing
anything to stop deforestation
Whole islands are on the brink
It is still making vast species of
fish, birds and wildlife extinct
This is a time of crisis when our
best minds need to come
together and think
Before the world as we know it
burns up and sink.

Time Zones- *King David Dunn*

I'm not as caught up as I move at the speed of light

Staying away from people that want to take flight

You want, you will, you might try to save your own life

Be that as it may- three Blacks died today

In time zones of their own construction

Not giving a damn about the deconstruction or the mayhem they

sowed

Saying what the blip, let's take another trip on the devil's mothership

Too smart for their own good

Fools totally misunderstood

You are entering a zone

Or another unleveled playing field

Where people shoot instead of talking about how they feel

Seeing the chaos on the next news reel

A 12-year-old girl died today

Fools shooting in a time zone where she had to stay.

Educate or Incarcerate – *Calvin T. Trahan*

Our kids suffer drastically from the lack of fight from the grass roots
We need to be pressing our Congressmen
Pushing them to fight for our youth
We gave 170 billion to Iraq to rebuild
Only to give 70 billion to our education system- this can't be real
This country is becoming a disgrace
It's a must we stand up and do something
Does anyone out there care about what our kids are becoming?
The schools in our communities are crumbling
Teachers being laid off in astronomical numbers
It's amazing how we can take care of someone else's kids
Only to neglect our own by taking their educational funding
Third grade test scores determine prison be space needed within the
next fourteen years
Teachers pressured by their principals to reach the sixty-five percent
passing rate for the STAAR test to keep their careers
The passion for teaching lost from the fighting for government
funding and hoping for contract extensions
They're under too much stress to even see our children's actual
learning potential
Unchallenged, improperly channeled frustration leads to a high rate
of dropout
The plan of destruction is coming into fruition directly in front of our
face without a doubt
No education leads to no future
More of the blind leading the blind

It's time we rise

It's time we unite

It's time we demand that none of our children be left behind

Prisons kill the family structure

They kill our communities

They kill all possibilities

Let's wage war against incarceration

By fighting diligently for our children's right to enhance their
capabilities

If we don't stand for anything else- let's stand for them

Let's push for education first;

to put their mass incarceration plan to an end

Educate don't incarcerate.

On Your Path
(Lord Keep Me)-
Deshaun

The devil constantly tries
to pull me down
But I know you've always
promised to be around
On your path, Lord keep
me.
The evil one wants to
make my life hell,
But under your protection
I'm sure things will go
well
On your path, Lord keep
me.
And though I'll make
some wrong turns along
the way

Your voice I'll always heed
and to your throne I'll
always pray
On your path, Lord keep
me.
Pure love you always
bring
So to you with joy I sing
On your path, Lord keep
me.
Though I may time to
time make a mistake
To right my wrong I vow
to do whatever it takes
On your path, Lord keep
me.
Amen.

Urban Specialist- *Damion Ford*

They say the hood is filled with

Hazardous **O**bstacles **O**f **D**estruction

It'll swallow you whole till you can't escape the suction

Some believe that sports and hip-hop are our only way out

Others feel that drugs, gangs and violence will give you the clout

Instant gratification keeps us going for months on end

It's the #1 downfall for our young Black men

Flipside to this hood story

Death or the pen

Life behind bars is not outside life

It's a legalized mechanism creating eternal slavery without the

possibility of freedom- and it's the truth

If this message doesn't evolve around you- it's for our youth

D. Ford had the right mindset but to some he still failed

His movement, his peers saw him derail and get jailed

Living that hard knock life, turning good into bad

Feeling like his drea-ms were shattered- thinking that the hood

was all he had

But God kept reaching, shining a light on his darkened path

His obstacles led to salvation when you sit down and do the math

He's a God of many chances- allowing you to be all that you can

be

Ask Obama, LeBron James

Ask Lecrae

Even ask Lucky

Fear no man but God

Glorify Him

Now THAT'S gangsta
Fifty wasn't referring to God but Ja'Rule
Calling him a wanksta
And for all you pistol packers and Bible slackers
Want a free invitation for God's guest list?
Grab you a seat at His round table
Become His disciple
And ponder this shout out to the Urban Specialist

.

Inmate Lives Matter- *C.W. Fleming*

We are the Divine Creation of God
Citizens of America and the children of man
This you must first understand
Our excessive immorality led to criminality
Thus we became wards of the state
Locked behind institutional gates
Labeled inmates; which supposedly justifies us being treated
with disdain and hate
Gassed, beaten, battered as if inmate lives don't matter

Being denied parole for a fight
When it was my manhood or my life
That ain't right

They deny lifers access to schools
Insist on us dumbing down and acting like fools
While manipulating us with their institutional rules
They themselves never follow the rules
Not even to give us privacy when we're on the stool
Viewing our naked bodies
Lusting on us that are hotties
And laughing about it at their parties
That ain't right
Never caring how we hurt
Only wanting more uncompensated work
Hiring haters to sit on horses and spit tobacco while we work
It gets sadder and I get madder cause inmate lives do matter.

We work hard and can't get a dime

Can't make parole after serving a hundred percent of our time

Our lives and families are miserable because they say we are

unredeemable and undesirable

On Wall Street we are a better investment than Angus beef

How cynical is it for them to give us religion as a treat

Then hide how many of us are dying from the heat

Have chronic diseases from the food that we eat

Leave suffering from prison PTSD- destined to repeat

It gets sadder because they believe that you believe that

Inmate lives don't matter

After doing time which is really hard

They still won't give us a job

Some of us have mad skills like Steve Jobs

Yet we are treated like hit men from the mob

The debt has been paid and we still can't get a McDonald's job

That's treating us worse than slobs

Like twenty years didn't matter

Like inmate lives don't matter

Orange is the new black

Black and brown are still filling the orange

Private prison profits are soaring

The prison industrial complex is roaring

About its safe prison and rape elimination act

All the time hiding the facts

About

It's inhumane acts

Perpetuated against the young and the old in Seg

Who's overly medicated with psychotropic meds

Who end up self-mutilated or dead

From the sheets on their own beds

Yeah- I know you never hear this chatter

Cause you've been fooled to believe that Inmate Lives *Don't*

Matter.

It's Kingdom WAR-

C.W. Fleming

From atop the steps of Babel
through the air waves the dragon
roars
The Leviathan has walked ashore
With The Angel's vial that causes
sores
Infecting scores
With no champion to protect the
poor
IT'S KINGDOM WAR
The Beast has appeared in the
East
He has caused peace to cease
The Gog and Magog have been
unleashed
Sodom and Gomorrah have
returned from beneath The Dead
Sea deep
War and rumors of war are on the
increase
IT'S KINGDOM WAR
The false prophets have come
together under the name of The
New World Interfaith Alliance
Six of the world's seven churches
have pledged complete
compliance
Our Church of Brotherly Love is
the only one still defiant

IT'S KINGDOM WAR
Pastors and Bishops are flickering
and falling like burned out stars
The masses have abandoned the
churches to frolic in bars
In the 'hood they are killing each
other for the rims off cars
IT'S KINGDOM WAR

Our children's eyes and ears are
being exposed and saturated with
porn
Our women are killing their babies
before they are even formed
The legislature says a baby doesn't
have the right to be born
IT'S KINGDOM WAR
Satan has sifted the politicians like
wheat
He has divided the masses based
on the hue of their feet
Because we suffer from national
hubris we can't admit moral
defeat
IT'S KINGDOM WAR
Pastors, sound the alarm for the
saints
To assemble and align without
regard for rank
Tell the leaders to call to order the
Circle of Kings –

And to prepare the Specialists to
go out in teams
Ask the First Ladies to tell them
on the prayer line that the
situation is urgent
And that all the prayers need to be
fervent
Tell the congregation it won't be
church as usual
There is no time for plays or
musicals
IT'S KINGDOM WAR

To successfully stand against the
Charismatic Charmer
We must all put on the full armor
We must be thankful that we are
saved
And be conscious of how it is we
behave
We must walk in the light
We must be aligned with the
thousand points of light
Never forgetting we are
representing
The TRUE Christ against the anti-
Christ
The Beast, Dragon and false
prophets all fear God's Word
It is the truth that will cause them
to all go mute

It's that seed in us that must bear
fruit
It is imperative that we raise the
bar
And live each day knowing who,
what and where we are
Because
IT'S KINGDOM WAR

He Is- C.W. Fleming

He is the **A**lmighty. The Absolute. My Avenger, Advisor Acceptor of repentance, Answerer of prayers. The Alpha who gave heaven its worth and the earth its dirt.

He is the **B**eneficent Blessed Blesser. The Bearer of Burdens; My Bridge over troubled water. The Bold, Blunt and Benevolent. He is the Breaker of strongholds, the Breath of life.

He is the **C**ompassionate Caretaker of every creature. The Celebrity's Celebrity, the Champions Champ, the Conqueror's Conqueror. The Composer of the symphony we call the universe.

He is the **D**efender of the weak. The Deliverer of the captives, the Designer of DNA, The Divine.

He is **E**lohim. The Exalted, Eternal, Everlasting. The Evolver of all that changes. The Energy source of all living cells. The Examiner of my heart. The Explainer of all mysteries. His Existence is Exquisite. His throne doth Extend over the heavens and the earth.

He is **F**aithful without Fault. The Father to the Fatherless who gives Favor. The Final say in all affairs. He is my Friend.

He is **G**od. The most Gracious. The Great. The Gatherer, the Guide. Our Gate to eternal peace who is Good all the time.

He is the **H**ope of the faithful. Hearer of the oppressed. The Helper of the righteous. The Healer of the sick.

He is **I**lluminating, Illustrious, The Immovable mover. The Impeccable, Impenetrable, Incomprehensible reality. My most Intimate companion.

He is **J**ehovah Nissi, Jehovah Rophe, Jehovah Shalom, Jehovah Jireh. He is the Just Judger of the Judges and the source of my Joy.

He is the **K**ing who is most Kind.

He is the **L**ight of the world. He Lives within my heart. He is LOVE.

He is My Master. My Maker; the Merciful one whose Mercy is renewed for me every day. He is the Music of my heart. He is the Mighty one whose strength never diminishes.

He is the **N**arrator of all truth; the Nurturer of my soul who is always near.

He is the **O**mniscient, Omnipresent, Omnipotent One. Overturner of sentences; Overrider of human laws, overseer of all of our lives whose presence is Overwhelming.

He is the **P**ardoner of sins, Preserver of safety, Penetrator of hearts. The Phenomenal Pure Power source who Protects and Provides. He is the source of Perfect Peace.

He is the **Q**uest of every sojourner of truth. The Questioner of every soul's intentions. He is Quick in punishment and even Quicker in granting forgiveness. He Quells rebellions, Quashes indictments and Quiets naysayers. He Qualified me when I was unqualified.

He is the **R**emitter of sins; the Redeemer of lives; the Reconciler of Relationships. He is the first Responder in times of need. He is the Refuge for the Rejected; the Remover of obstacles; the Restorer, Rewarder, Revealer of secrets and schemes. He is Rich so much that He owns the planets.

He is my **S**hepherd, my Staff that I lean on when I'm tired. He is My Sustainer and my Savior; the Secret that keeps me going.

He is The **T**ruth. The Thesis statement of all my talks.

He is **U**naltered, Unbeaten, Unbroken and the Ultimate reality. He is the **V**erifier of good deeds whose vastness cannot be seen or measured.

He is the **W**onder of the World.
The Watcher who sees every grain
of sand under every rock on every
planet in the universe.
He is **X**enial and never leaves us
outside.
He is the **Y**oke-destroying yielder
of truth.
He is **Z**ealous to point us towards
Zion because that is just the way
that He is.
He is **A**wesome, the **B**est, the
Curer of whatever ails you.
HE IS!
Do you know Him?

OG Come Back- *Ata The Lion*

OG did you see the news?
The lights were flashing on the
Red and Blues
As the chopper filmed with a
bird's eye view
The question the whole hood
asked, *"Where were you?"*

When Brodrick grabbed his block
to blast, a Phantom enemy you
taught him in the past.

You've left the hood living good, a
real change that's misunderstood
by a new generation that considers
your life soul food.

Living by ya' code in "G-MODE"
Step by step down the same road
thinking they'll find the Mother
load
Of trills that will make them feel
justified for their kills if they don't
die in the field doing a bad deal for
fake ex-pills.

You know this spiel
It's what made you ill

The reason why you stopped
spinning the games suicidal wheel.

A decade has passed and still
another generation is falling fast:
Poor/young/dropouts; brown and
blacks you know the cast so we
ask; OG will you come back to tell
the truth to the youth? Your new
life is a fruit, but you've gone mute
in your True Religion suit.

Like you don't hear the pain of the
mothers
The Blood Cry of your own slain
brother and the children please to
stop the violence from going any
further.

OG you should be in the grave or a
slave in a concrete cave.
You didn't survive the game
because you are brave-
It was because of Grace
That's the only reason you beat
the case
To keep your life from being a
waste- come back to the place
where everyone knows your face
and tell them that they too can
receive GRACE.

OG you know I'm spitting true
facts
Don't turn your back- COME
BACK!
Not to film those still stuck in
traps
But to clean up this crap by giving
back.
OG COME BACK!
OG COME BACK!

Poems for Our Children

Thank You- *Jeff McClendon*
Dedicated to my two beautiful
daughters Symone & Aaliyah

If I had one chance to express my
gratitude and how much you
mean to me, I'd say thank you for
your unconditional love and for
always believing in me.

You've always been by my side
and you are truly my biggest
inspiration.
I never want to let you down
again, coming home to you is my
motivation.

You have both grown up over the
years and turned out to be
beautiful young ladies.
When I really think about it I get
sad and ask what happened to my
babies?

I couldn't ask for two better
daughters- I'm so proud to call
you mine.
I can't wait to get home to show
you- it's just a matter of time.

Symone, you're in high school now
and you're starting to get
interested in boys.
I wish I could reverse time- I
would still have you playing with
toys.

Aaliyah, you're in the fourth grade
and still like Doc McStuffins.
You told me you wanted to be a
chef so you could bake me some
muffins.

I love it when we talk on the
phone. Our conversations are a
blast.
You both are so funny, I can't do
nothing but smile and laugh.

All three of us have so much in
common- we even like to eat our
vegetables.
We all have the same little nose
and I even gave you my freckles.

Thank you so much for not being a
judge.
And for always forgiving me and
not holding a grudge.

It takes a lot of strength to stay
down with your daddy.
Believe me when I get the chance I
will return the favor gladly.

You mean the world to me, words
can't express how I truly feel.
But as long as our hearts are
connected we know the feelings
are real.

Every time I try to say I'm sorry
you say, "Don't worry about it dad
we all make mistakes."
Your unconditional love gives me
enough tears to fill up the Great
Lakes.

I hope one day you'll both read
this and understand what I'm
trying to do.
It's simply to say two words that
hard to explain-
Thank you!

A Father's Love- *Damion Ford*

From the inside of a prison cell all
I can do is ponder
Things that seemed to bring me
happiness no longer
From the day I first saw your face
I wanted nothing but the best for
you   •
I changed your diapers, I bathed
your body and clothed you- and
made sure you ate no matter what
From inside of a prison cell all I
can do is ponder
Will my son or daughter
experience a prison sentence like
their father
So rebellious
Just like me when I was younger
Head up, chest out, full of pride
like no other
I didn't raise you to disrespect, I
encouraged you to do better
I can feel your pain and hurt
I apologize for my absence
Even though I'm locked in the
pen- I live a life of freedom
You're free to be what you want to
be
Just let me lead you

A doctor, lawyer or maybe even a
policeman
No matter what you chose it's
possible to achieve it
I ask for your forgiveness for
leaving you unattended
I love you like your mother
Our love is never ending

Surround yourself with people
that care for your greatest interest
I'm on my knees constantly
praying for you to feel this at best

God is really real
So I offer nothing but realness
As your father, I stand strong as a
pillar holding up buildings

If I Had a Child- *Kielyn Reed*

If I had a child;
It would be my duty to make them
smile everyday of their lives.
I would tell them to hold on to joy
no matter what life throws their
way. I would encourage them to
always have a free mind and never
get to old to play.

If I had a child;
I would show them love in hopes
that they would understand its
power. I would teach them to
appreciate every moment in order
to make the best out of every hour.
If I had a child;
I would tell them to hold on to
their innocence and to keep all of
their dreams. I would tell them to
never allow mistakes to stop them
from doing anything.

If I had a child;
I would tell them to never stop
asking questions, looking for or
seeking truth. I would show them
how most grownups got lost in life
because they forgot the things
they learned in their youth.

If I had a child;
I would show them how a natural
high was better than any drug on
earth. I would tell them that when
they get high they will forget their
precious and priceless worth.

If I had a child;
I would teach them that most
bullies lack love. That's why they
ridicule, threaten, push and shove.
What they really need is a kiss, a
friendly hug and to know that they
are accepted and loved.

If I had a child;
I would tell them that their
thoughts, likes and wants will
shape the future world. I would
start them to thinking how they
could make this world better for
every boy and girl.

If I had a child;
I would tell them that the more
you give love, the more love will
exist. It's only through love the
world's problems can be fixed.

If I had a child;
I would warn them of the evil that
lurks and creeps. I would tell
about the danger of gangs and the
streets.

If I had a child;
I would tell them that education is
the key to determine their fate. I
would tell them to stay in school
to become great.

But I don't have a child.
Why?
Because I got locked up as a child
and have spent all of my life in a
cage.
I never finished high school, went
to a prom or even a dance.
This is why if I had a child I would
beg them to listen to me so that
they would have all the things it
takes to stay free.

Fatherless Son- *Melvin Davis*

Some people used to tell me, "You
remind me of your dad."
But they reminded me of someone
I never had
How could I love someone I have
never known?
Whose only words ever to me
were, "You're a man you can make
it on your own."
Doesn't a seed have the right to
grow into a tree?
To be told its loved and
encouraged to be the best it could
be.
From the start I was finished, no
rite of passage was given
I always felt like a menace and
never had nobody to listen.
For me it was like no one cared
I ended up in prison, that's how I
faired.
Because I was fatherless,
knowledge and wisdom were
never shared.
Because we are both fatherless
this knowledge I freely share.
Trust me, I know how you feel and
how rough life can be

But don't sell your soul to the
Illuminati because the game
comes with an un-repayable fee.
Remember that having your mom
will always be your best blessing
Don't ever forget her life lessons.
Be obedient to her and you won't
be stressing.
Young man, take this to heart.
To be strong is to stand alone.
To be smart is to be apart from
everything wrong.
For sure you're going to make
some mistakes and may even fall.
But when you do, lift yourself up
and with pride stand tall.
Always let your yes mean yes and
your no mean no.
Think for yourself and choose wise
men to follow.
Stand your ground even when
you're afraid,
And always remember that fear is
not something God has made.
Love the people who treat you
right.
And know that evil does creep in
the streets after midnight.
Just because you don't have a
daddy, is not an excuse for you not
to be happy.

Don't ever listen to anybody who tell you what you can't be Lil Man. Cause you can do all things through Christ, Yes you can , yes you can!

Daddy Why?- *Keilyn Reed*

When I left you were a baby and your mother told me all you did was cry. Now that you're a teenager you ask me, Daddy why? At first you were too young, but now it's time for me to tell all that was done.

You asked me why did I abandon you when you needed me the most?

Baby girl you will not get an excuse- only the truth

And the truth is I was trying to take the short cuts to buying you the world.

I hear you say that "Daddy I didn't want your gifts, I only wanted you."

To that I must tell you that before you were born, I lived a life that wasn't right. I was in the game and gangs.

When you were born and I had to provide like a real man, I found it hard to change.

That's the real cause for all your childhood pain, I psyched myself out to believe that I had to provide for you and your mother by any means necessary and committed a lot of crimes that weren't necessary.

I hear you ask me, "Daddy, why should I forgive you now?"

Baby girl I don't want you to forgive me for me. I want you to forgive me for yourself.

Baby girl if you don't let go of your hate for me, you'll remain bitter, upset and angry.

It's not your fault that I cheated, stole, sold drugs and got caught. I did those crimes and now I am doing my time.

But you have nothing in front of you but a good life.

You'll graduate college and make a lot of money an become the next President's wife.

I had to make my mistakes and finally get it right.

And my mistakes caused you to grow up in pain. For that, I will forever be ashamed.

Please forgive me for you'll be happier when you do.

I hear you say, "Daddy, I really need you in my life now because I feel so unloved."

Second chances are often times better than the first.

I'll get it right and make sure that I'm never again the cause of your hurt.

I will teach you that your self-love is what gives you worth.

It's your beauty within that will cause you to win.

And your beauty within has always been great.

You just need to increase it with faith.

I know life without your father seems so unfair, but please believe that I have always loved you and do care.

I know I missed your childhood and that ain't right.

But my daddy days are not over for you-

Cause I will be your daddy for life.

I Just- *Jeff McClendon*

I just lie in bed thinking about the
two of you.
Just wishing that this dream
would soon come true.
I just want to hold you in my arms
and keep you close.
I just want you to know that I miss
you- my children the most.
I just hope you understand how
deep and unconditional my love is
for you .
I just can't wait until we can go to
the restaurant and eat our favorite
foods.
I just sit here and smile when I
think about all the wonderful
times we had together.
I close my eyes and imagine that
this thought will last forever.
Sometimes I just cry when I think
how long we've been apart.
And at other times I just feel so
blessed because of the love that
runs deep in my heart.
I just believe that this was all part
of the plan.
We just have to believe and put
our faith in His hands.

I just hope that we will always be
best friends and never treat each
other mean.
I just know that together were are
an unstoppable and unbreakable
team.
I just know that when I come
home it will be better than in the
beginning.
I just know that just like a fairytale
this is gonna end with the perfect
ending.

I Will- *Jeff McClendon*

I will be your father and teacher,
someone who can give you the
right direction.
I will be your mountain- big,
strong and tall who you can come
to for protection.
I will give you all my knowledge
and love.
Something we both know comes
from God above.
I will cherish your unconditional
love.
I promise to love you from the
bottom of my soul.
My adoration of you is very hard
to control
I will take the time to give you the
attention that you need.
I will take you on your first date
and show you how a young lady is
supposed to be treated.
I will give you a shoulder to lean
on when challenges have you
confused.
I will give you the game so you
won't go out and choose the wrong
dude.
I will never turn my back on you.

I will always be a very loyal and
dedicated dad.
I will be your friend to the end
through good times and bad.
I will be like a mirror- look in it
and see your own reflection.
You'll also be looking at the one
who gets all my love and affection.
I will always be there for you.
Always.
No matter what.

I'll Be Home Before You're 10- C.W. Fleming

Your blouse is pink and your jeans are blue

Don't ever cry thinking that daddy doesn't see you.

Because I always do.

Your grades are all A's and you still don't like peas.

You told your grandmother that you wanted to sail The Seven Seas.

At first it was because of the mermaid- now it's because of Nemo.

You are my princess and I love you so so so!

Your mother told me that you pray for me every night.

The angels came to tell me that you are doing everything right.

Princess keep doing your best and remember that Jesus is your friend.

I promise you that I'll be home before you are ten.

Kisses, kisses and slobber!

Love Always,

Your Father

My Mini Me- *T. Byrd*

You're my mini me.

You're all I think about day in and day out.

What hurts me the most is not being there to teach you how to be a man.

And to help you understand that in life everything don't always go as planned.

I apologize for not being there to pick you up when you're down;

and to console you when you were scared of that clown.

I apologize for missing your first day of school; and for not being there to tell you that it ain't cool violating school rules.

I thank you for listening to my words.

I want you to grow up to protect and serve- always knowing that you are a Byrd.

I want you to do well in school and have good test scores.

I want you to know that the mistakes I made are not yours.

I want you to help people and do right; and know and believe that when I come home you will have a good life.

You have my nose, chin, muscles and now I want you to have my wisdom.

Do the right thing.

Make good choices and don't ever do anything to come to prison.

Love Always,
Daddy

Baby Girl- L. Brown

When your mother told me that she was pregnant with you, my child, I
looked up toward heaven and smiled.
One side for me was so elated.
The other side of me was discombobulated.
I was frustrated facing a prison bid which I hated.

Baby Girl,
I was going through a storm and my life seemed so worn.
I was hoping to be free long enough to see you born.
The thoughts of not being able to see you come into the world had me torn.

Baby Girl,
One day when I was doing time behind these walls, I was surprised with a
special letter at mail call.
I opened the letter- received your picture and began to bawl.
I told everybody look. Look at her she looks just like me sitting all pretty like
in her stroller.
I thought, "My what I wouldn't give to be there to hold her."

Baby Girl,
Every day I showed your pictures to all of my friends. When they told me how
beautiful you were all I could do was grin.
It made me feel so good cause you looked like my twin.

Baby Girl,
I remember walking into the visiting room and to my surprise who did I see?
It was you, my baby girl, smiling back looking at me.
When we first met I was so nervous my knees were clacking.

Mama had smiling tears falling from her eyes and was clapping.

In the back of my mind I was thanking God for making that day happen.

In visitation we're all smiles and carrying on.

You looked at me with a tear in your eye and asked me, "Daddy when are you coming home?"

Baby Girl,

Butterflies turned in my stomach as everyone became quiet.

This was the painful reality and I could no longer deny it.

Mama looked at me and asked me was I okay? I nodded my head as I contemplated what to say.

Baby Girl,

This is the vicinity that's housing me for a while.

This is where I will be for now. The Lord will bring us through this somehow.

Dry your eyes and give me a kiss. Let's enjoy this moment because of its bliss.

You are my world.

You're what keeps me trying to get back to that world.

I love you with all my heart

Baby Girl.

Dad I'm Dating- *C.W. Fleming*

When I got arrested you were just being weaned.

Now you've grown into this witty and wise teen ready to enter the dating scene.

Rule Number 1,

Make sure your date isn't mean.

Dating is the process by which you make an acquaintance a friend.

Dating is not an occasion for you to participate in carnal sin.

Always show your date grace, kindness and favor.

Needless to say, I expect you to be on your best behavior.

When you are around a young lady and your butterflies start to flutter,

Make sure you respect her the same way I have always respected your mother.

At the end of the date, look at the girl's chin

If the date was good she will be sporting a grin- which means you'll be able to go out with her again.

Plan your next date to be a journey to explore something that's fun.

Then enjoy talking about the things that you have done- together.

Follow the first date up with a card and a letter.

Son, thanks for asking for my advice.

I have complete faith in you.

Make your first date special and nice.

Love Always,

Your Father

Stay Connected...

Website: www.cwflemingbooks.com
Email: cwflemingwrites@gmail.com
Blog: www.thestrengthtolove.com

Other Books by C.W. Fleming...

∞ Elephant Valley: Love Tested

∞ Jesus Christ in the Criminal Justice System

∞ Jesus Christ in the Criminal Justice System: _Restoring Justice_

　Edition

Made in the USA
Monee, IL
17 June 2021